100 Ideas for Primary Teachers:

Numeracy Difficulties and Dyscalculia

Other titles in the 100 Ideas for Primary Teachers series

Other titles by Patricia Babtie

100 Ideas for Primary Teachers:

Numeracy Difficulties and Dyscalculia

Patricia Babtie

B L O O M S B U R Y

LONDON • OXFORD • NEW YORK • NEW DELHI • SYDNEY

Bloomsbury Education
An imprint of Bloomsbury Publishing Plc

50 Bedford Square
London
WC1B 3DP
UK

1385 Broadway
New York
NY 10018
USA

www.bloomsbury.com

Bloomsbury is a registered trade mark of Bloomsbury Publishing Plc

First published 2017

British Library Cataloguing-in-Publication Data
A catalogue record for this book is available from the British Library.

ISBN:
PB 9781441169730
ePub 9781441121967
ePDF 9781441192486

Library of Congress Cataloging-in-Publication Data
A catalog record for this book is available from the Library of Congress.

10 9 8 7 6 5 4 3 2 1

Typeset by Newgen Knowledge Works (P) Ltd., Chennai, India
Printed and bound in the UK by CPI Group (UK) Ltd, Croydon CR0 4YY

This book is produced using paper that is made from wood grown in managed, sustainable forests. It is natural, renewable and recyclable. The logging and manufacturing processes conform to the environmental regulations of the country of origin.

To view more of our titles please visit www.bloomsbury.com

Contents

Acknowledgements

I am grateful to so many people for their expertise, encouragement and enthusiasm. It seems invidious to mention some and not all. However with the limits of space, I can single out only a few. My interest in dyscalculia started at Emerson House where the late Dorian Yeo taught me about the magic of the dot patterns and Jane Emerson and I wrote several books. Emeritus Professor Brian Butterworth's explanations of dyscalculia made the significance of early counting clear to me, and Professor Diana Laurillard turned some of the basic games into digital activities.

Most of my work has been in schools, particularly at the amazingly supportive St Richard's CE Primary School, Richmond, though I have taught adults with numeracy difficulties as well. Teaching colleagues Sue Dillon, Angela King, Siock Kheng Ang, Ludi Evangelista, Charlotte Chase, Jane Trapmore and Emma Fullerton have all challenged and improved my thinking. Occupational therapist Tracey Le Roux, shared her expertise on how to improve underlying skills and allowed me to quote from her website (Idea 5). Perhaps the people to whom I owe the most are the pupils. It has been so exciting to watch fear of numbers turn into enjoyment and competence. Thank you to everyone who has made that possible.

Finally, thank you to Miriam Davey and Emily Wilson, my editors at Bloomsbury. Emily's organisation, incisive comments and deft 'red pen' made the writing process rewarding too.

Introduction

The ideas in this book are practical, simple and straightforward to do. They are designed to develop numerical understanding and flexible thinking. Pupils with numeracy difficulties need time to explore basic concepts. For them, counting to 10 is neither simple nor straightforward. Even those who find this easy can learn a great deal by exploring the relationships between the first ten numbers. Concepts of partitioning, commutativity, and inverse relationships emerge from activities with small numbers. Later there are investigations of the principle of exchange before moving on to multi-digit numbers, multiplication, place value and standard methods as well as considering the difference between number tracks (counting numbers) and number lines (measuring numbers)

The games and activities are designed to encourage active learning. All have been tried and tested in classrooms with small groups and individual pupils. Pupils use equipment to model numbers, then discuss them, draw diagrams and write numbers and equations. This method is known as multi-sensory learning and can be summarised as 'concrete – diagrammatic – symbolic'. Evidence from neuroscience supports this approach as there is a close connection between numerical thinking and action. Visualisation is a particularly important part of numeracy, so ensure that pupils handle objects and draw diagrams in order to establish strong visual memories.

Readers may be surprised that the book starts with ideas for improving motor movement and general perceptual skills as well as the language associated with them. Difficulties with spatial orientation, rhythm and timing are sometimes overlooked when pupils have numeracy difficulties, yet they profoundly affect the ability to understand instructions and organise thoughts. There is also a pernicious belief in the Western world that some people can't learn maths because they are born bad at numbers. This is not true – apart from those with dyscalculia.

Numeracy difficulties arise for many reasons, including perceptual immaturity or specific learning difficulties such as dyscalculia, dyslexia and ADD (attention deficit disorder). About five percent of people are born with a number 'deficit' known as dyscalculia. It is characterised by an inability to subitize, which is the ability to compare small quantities instantly. If you put out two groups of objects, one containing two items and the other with four items, a person with dyscalculia cannot see that there is a difference between them. (It probably has an evolutionary origin because animals, birds and fish can do it.) As you may imagine, if you cannot do this, learning to calculate is impossible. Pupils with dyscalculia have to be patiently taught to count before they can move on.

The biggest obstacle to learning is fear. Children develop at different rates, physically, perceptually and cognitively, and this affects the speed with which they progress in the classroom. Unfortunately the effect of rushing young pupils can be catastrophic. Repeated failure and humiliation quickly turns to anxiety and fear, a state in which the brain shuts down so the pupil cannot learn.

Overcome anxiety by ensuring that pupils start at the point they can understand and then learn to enjoy numbers. Getting pleasure from number activities encourages them to do more and develop competence and confidence. So don't rush. Let your pupils have fun exploring. Indeed, evidence from neuroscience suggests that having fun stimulates the brain's reward system in ways that can accelerate learning.

Websites

The Internet provides an apparently inexhaustible supply of ideas. A few of my favourite websites are:

www.number-sense.co.uk

www.nrich.maths.org

www.ot-mom-learning-activities.com

www.educationalneuroscience.org.uk

How to use this book

This book includes quick, easy, practical ideas and guidance for you to dip in and out of to help you provide for pupils with numeracy difficulties or who have dyscalculia.

Each idea includes:

- a catchy title, easy to refer to and share with your colleagues
- a quote from a practitioner, parent or child describing their experience that has led to the idea
- a summary of the idea in bold, making it easy to flick through the book and identify an idea you want to use at a glance
- a step-by-step guide to implementing the idea.

Each idea has a symbol next to it

- an information symbol denotes that the idea contains general information about the topic
- a time symbol indicates approximately how long the idea is likely to take, however these are only a rough guide as pupils with difficulties may need considerably longer.

     information

     less than 10 minutes

     about 15 minutes

     about 30 minutes

     about 45 minutes

Each idea also includes one or more of the following:

Teaching tip	Taking it further	Bonus idea
Practical tips and advice for how and how not to run the activity or put the idea into practice.	Ideas and advice for how to extend the idea or develop it further.	There are 23 bonus ideas in this book that are extra-exciting, extra-original and extra-interesting.

Online resources also accompany this book. Those for specific ideas are referenced in the activity instructions in the book. There are also templates for you to print out the cards for many of the ideas in the book:

- number cards: 0–10 and 11–20
- dot pattern cards: 1–10
- number word cards: zero–twenty.

All online resources can be found at www.bloomsbury.com/100-ideas-primary-dyscalculia.

Share how you use these ideas and find out what other practitioners have done using **#100ideas**.

Numeracy basics

Part 1

Daily number

▷

"Did you catch an interesting number today?"

Introduce a 'daily number' along the lines of 'show and tell'. Pupils can take it in turns to tell the class about a number they found and what the question it answers is.

Encourage pupils to notice numbers they meet in their daily lives and share them with the class. Numbers are everywhere, from the pages in a book to scores on the football field; from the time on the clock to the number on the door. Numbers have different functions – not all are to do with counting and measuring. Some, such as your mobile phone number, are simply used to identify something in the same way that a name does. Numbers are used to answer questions such as: How many? How big? How far? How old? What time?

- The number diary – each pupil keeps a number diary: they look for numbers in their world outside school (at home, at the shops and on their way to school). They write one number in their diary every day with a short description of where they found the number and what information it gave.
- The daily number – pupils take it in turns to share a favourite or interesting number with the class every day. The pupil writes the number on the board and tells the class where they found it. The class suggests the kind of questions that the number might be the answer to. Write the questions on the board and discuss them.

What is a number?

"Data drives the world and it all starts with counting."

Think of a number and you think of a symbol. A range of concepts are compressed into the symbol that represents the idea that is number.

Human beings developed numbers to make sense of the world – a world which today extends from the sub-atomic to the entire universe.

The concept of number has to be learned by experiencing things; it cannot be merely transmitted as a series of symbols and procedures. Neuroscientists have discovered that mathematical understanding is rooted in the perceptual and motor systems of the body. Initially pupils use number words as adjectives to describe what they see, e.g. four cats. Gradually they learn to abstract the concept of the number four as an abstract idea – what is sometimes referred to as the 'fourness' of four.

The word 'number' denotes:

- a numerosity – the total quantity in a collection of objects
- a numeral – the word and symbol representing the numerosity
- a digit – the term used for the numerals 0 to 9 from which all numbers are formed
- a multi-digit number – the value of each digit depends on its position in the number.

Pupils need to understand numbers in order to use them to solve problems. Work with small numbers to build secure foundations and teach pupils to reason about the relationships between numbers and the structures within them.

> **Teaching tip**
>
> Pupils need to enjoy learning about numbers. Fear and anxiety disrupt brain signals and can persist for a lifetime.

Numerosity curiosity

"Can you instantly see how many there are? Birds do it. Fish do it. I do it. You do it. Some people can't do it."

Test whether pupils can quickly distinguish the difference between two small quantities of objects.

Humans (and animals) are born with the ability to subitize, which means they can quickly tell whether two small quantities contain the same number of objects, or that they are different. 'Small' means up to about four or five. People with dyscalculia are unable to distinguish the relative size of small groups in this way. Nor can they instantly recognise how many there are if they are shown two or three objects.

This activity for two players will flag up any potential problem. It also gives pupils practice in counting a few objects.

- Each player has five counters hidden in a secret store, e.g. a mug or small bag. The counters must all be the same colour and the same size. Glass nuggets are ideal.
- Both players take a few counters. They place their hands on the table, taking care to keep the counters hidden.
- One player says, 'Show', and both players quickly display their counters.
- Players race to touch the larger quantity and say: 'Bigger.'
- If the quantities are the same, the players must touch both quantities and say: 'Same.'
- The winner is the first player to touch the correct quantity.
- Each player counts the number of objects in their own pile before returning them to their store.

Taking it further

Once pupils can count accurately, they can say the number of counters in the larger pile rather than simply pointing. The first person to say the number is the winner.

Directional language

"Teacher said: 'Draw a line across the page.' Ivan very carefully drew a large X (a cross)."

Use body movement to make sense of directional language that will help pupils understand instructions.

Some pupils cannot follow instructions because they have difficulty understanding directional language such as the words *in, on, under, behind, in front, next to, across, above, below, left, right* etc. These words play an essential part in comprehension. Their meaning is closely associated with the motor systems of the body, so get pupils moving.

Do these exercises for a few minutes a day. Pupils stand comfortably, arms by their sides. The teacher gives an instruction, the pupils repeat the instruction, and then carry it out. The movements must be definite and accurate. Pupils return to the starting position after each instruction.

- Single instruction, e.g. 'Point up.' (Or down, in front, behind, to the side . . .) 'Stand behind the chair.' 'Stand next to someone.' 'Show me your left hand.' 'Stamp your right foot.'
- Two instructions, e.g. 'Take one step forward and then sit down.' 'Take two steps back then clap your hands.' 'Step forward and then take one step to the right.'
- Multiple instructions, e.g. 'Put your right hand on your head and your left hand on your left foot.' 'Put your right hand on your right shoulder and your left hand on your right knee.' (This instruction involves crossing the midline of the body. This is extremely difficult for pupils with directional and spatial difficulties. Work on improving motor movement as discussed in Ideas 5, 6 and 7.)

Teaching tip

Check that pupils can identify their right and left hands. Always start by asking pupils to show their left hand. The reason is that they often interpret the word 'right' as meaning the hand that they 'write' with. So a left-handed pupil may raise their left hand in response to the instruction to show their right hand.

Never demonstrate right and left when you are facing pupils. The mirror image confuses them.

Be cautious about giving instructions that cross the midline of the body until pupils are ready (see Idea 5).

Elbow tickle

"I didn't realise how difficult this can be for some children."

Spend a few minutes each day crossing the midline to improve co-ordination and spatial awareness.

This simple exercise helps pupils learn to cross the midline. This ability is important for developing spatial awareness which has an important role in stimulating brain activity and enabling us to understand the world in relation to our own bodies. Pupils who have difficulties in this area may appear clumsy, or be unable to follow instructions.

'The midline is an imaginary line drawn from the head to the feet that separates the left and the right halves of the body. Crossing the midline means that a body part (e.g. hand or foot) is able to easily move over to the other side of the body to work there. Being able to do this is important for brain development as well as physical development.' (Tracey Le Roux, Occupational therapist)

Do this activity a few times at spare moments during the day until pupils can do it easily. It is physically impossible to tickle your elbow without crossing the midline.

- Working individually, ask pupils to sit comfortably with arms relaxed on the table.
- Explain and demonstrate how to use one hand to tickle the elbow on the other arm.
- Pupils tickle one elbow, then put their arms back on the table before tickling the other elbow.
- If a pupil cannot do this action themselves, gently guide their hand to the elbow.

Arm swing

"Look! Now I can do it on my own." (Excited eight-year-old who chose to practise at home.)

People are often surprised to learn that a basic sense of rhythm and body movement plays an important role in developing numerical thinking (as well as reading and writing).

Most children learn to synchronise movement and sound as they develop. Those who have difficulties doing this need to be taught how, as poor rhythm and timing can affect language processing and comprehension. Pupils need to proceed at their own pace developing a steady rhythm and crossing the midline. (See Idea 5 for information on the midline.)

- Ask pupils to sit comfortably in a chair with their back supported and both feet flat on the floor.
- They adopt the starting position by placing their hands on their shoulders.
- They move one hand to touch their opposite knee, and say, 'Knee', as they touch their knee. (If a pupil has difficulty, the teacher touches the hand lightly and guides it to the opposite knee.)
- They return to the starting position and say, 'Shoulder', when their hand touches their shoulder.
- Do the same activity with the other hand.
- Pupils continue the activity using alternating hands for about ten repetitions, developing a steady rhythm. They do not hurry.

Encourage them to practise this activity every day. Even when they can do it, it is important to continue saying 'Knee' and 'Shoulder' in time with the action. Note that the language is restricted to the words 'shoulder' and 'knee'. Do not use the terms 'right' and 'left'.

> **Teaching tip**
>
> Learning to accomplish this is a terrific boost to confidence. Pupils quickly realise that they are getting better and are delighted when they finally master the task. It also proves a great motivator as they discover that through practice and perseverance they can do something they thought they could not. Remind pupils of this when they get stuck on numerical problems.

Tick tock

"Knees up, arms out gets the day off to a good start."

Rhythm and timing are fundamental pre-learning skills. Practising precision movements helps improve a range of cognitive functions including auditory processing, concentration and memory as well as motor coordination.

In this activity pupils develop a rhythmic movement as they swing one arm and touch the hand to the raised knee on the opposite side of their body. They say, 'Tick, tock', to help keep in time.

Basic activity: pupils need to stand for this activity with sufficient space to swing their arms without hitting each other. It is important to work steadily and not allow the pupils to rush. The aim is control, accuracy and rhythm, not speed. Give the instructions one at a time and continue the activity for one minute.

- Stand with your arms outstretched at shoulder height.
- Raise your left knee.
- Swing your right arm across your body and touch your left knee with your right hand. Say 'Tick'.
- Return to starting position with both feet on the floor and arms outstretched.
- Raise your right knee.
- Swing your left arm across your body and touch your right knee with your left hand. Say 'Tock'.

Advanced activity: pupils line up one behind the other. The pupil at the head of the line starts the tick tock movement learnt above and sets the pace with crisp, easy to follow movements. Each pupil joins in in turn until they are all keeping time. The initial efforts are likely to be rather ragged but with practice they will become more co-ordinated.

Bonus Idea ★

A line dance consists of a repeated sequence of steps performed by a group of people who stand in a line. Challenge pupils to develop their own dance by devising a new sequence of arm movements and steps that they all learn to do simultaneously, e.g. kick a leg up behind them and touch the foot with the opposite hand. Ask other pupils to provide a simple clapping rhythm and they will quickly have an impressive display for assembly.

Pattern practice

"When you want a thing done, don't do it yourself; persuade the pupils to do it."

Order colours and shapes to make sequences and patterns.

Pupils need to be conscious of patterns in non-numerical situations before they can understand patterns and relationships in mathematics. In these exercises, pupils order objects or shapes to form a sequence, and describe the sequence. Once they can do that they repeat the sequence to form a pattern.

> **Bonus Idea** ★
>
> Give pupils a simple line pattern on isometric paper (see online resources) and ask them to continue the pattern. Ask them to describe the pattern.

Colour

- Put three different coloured counters in a line and draw and colour a diagram of the sequence.
- Describe the order and write it down, e.g.

  'The order is red, green, yellow.'

- Rearrange the counters to form a different order. Describe the order and write it down again.
- How many different ways can you order three colours?
- Choose one of the sequences and repeat it several times to make a pattern.
- Draw the pattern, e.g.

Shape

Draw three different shapes in a line, e.g. a circle, a square and a triangle.

Follow the same routine as that done with the colours.

Barrier games

"See things from another person's point of view."

Pupils hone their communication skills by giving instructions so that someone else can replicate a model or a drawing they have made.

Successful communication depends on expressing your thoughts clearly and accurately so that someone else grasps the meaning you intend to convey. Doing it well is not easy, as anyone who has ever had an argument will confirm.

Communication starts with an idea that is then transmitted using language. The message may be compressed into symbols as in maths or music, or sculpture, or diagrams. However all can be described using spoken language. In this activity pupils give each other instructions to draw a model, or replicate a diagram. Then they compare the results and discuss the similarities and differences and how the description could have been improved.

Coloured counters

Two pupils sit side by side and erect a barrier between them so they cannot see each other's work. Players take turns to give and receive instructions about a display of coloured counters.

- Player A puts out four coloured counters and describes the arrangement, e.g. 'There are four counters in a line. They are red, blue, green and yellow.'
- Player B places four counters in a row in the same colour order.
- The players remove the barrier and compare the displays and discuss the results.

Player A   Player B

In the example above, Player A did not specify the direction of the line – it could be vertical, horizontal or diagonal. The distance between counters was also not mentioned – are they spread out or do they touch each other?

Draw a mugwump

Pupils enjoy imaginary figures. Start by creating imaginary figures using a simple sequence of shapes such as circle, square, star and, later, progress to more complex designs. Players take turns to give and receive instructions.

- Player A draws an imaginary character called a mugwump and describes it to Player B who draws their interpretation of the description, e.g. 'Pat is a mugwump. Its body is a rectangle. The neck is round and it has a square head. There is one oval eye. It has three star-shaped feet. It has no arms but there is one hand which grows out of its head.'
- Remove the barrier and compare the displays.

Player A   Player B

This example should provide plenty of opportunity for discussion. The orientation of the rectangle is not mentioned, nor is the relative size of the head, neck and body. Does the hand attach to the top or one side of the head?

Taking it further

Clear and accurate use of language is vital both for communicating ideas to others and clarifying them for yourself. Extend the use of barrier games to more complex situations such as Secret sequences (Idea 43).

Learning to look

"Tell me what you see. It will change the way you look at the world."

Use puzzles and games to sharpen visual perceptual skills.

The visual image plays a central role in communicating information. From letters and numbers, to pictures and graphs, visual images are everywhere. Understanding and interpreting these images depends on visual perception – the way the brain analyses and organises what the eyes see. Visual perceptual skills develop as a child matures.

Components of visual perception include:

- visual discrimination – identify similarities and differences
- figure ground – focus on one shape or item and ignore what is irrelevant
- spatial relations – identify different shapes and understand distance
- visual closure – recognise an object when only part is visible
- form constancy – recognise objects even when the size or the orientation has changed.

Visual discrimination plays a key role in academic success. Improve these skills through 'find the odd one out' and 'spot the difference' activities. Pupils talk about what they see and describe similarities and differences. It is the combined force of vision and language that produce brain changes that improve visual perception and memory.

Find the odd one out

- Show the pupils a set of simple odd one out images (stars from this activity are available online).
- Pupils name the objects in the picture and describe them.

- They explain what is the same about them.
- They find the object that is different and explain why it is different.

Spot the difference

- Find or create two simple spot the difference pictures (dogs from this activity are available online).
- Pupils describe the picture.
- They focus on individual parts of the picture and explain what is the same and what is different in each part on the two versions.
- They then draw the missing items on the picture.

What's missing?

- Put a selection of objects on a tray. Vary the number of objects according the age and ability of the pupils.
- The pupils look at them and name each object.
- Cover the objects with a cloth and secretly remove one object.
- Uncover the tray and ask the pupils what is missing.

Taking it further

There are plenty of free printable resources available on the Internet. Search for images of 'Spot the difference' and 'Find the odd one out'. Or, teach pupils to prepare their own 'Find the difference' puzzles. Encourage them to be inventive and see how many different types of diagrams and pictures they can produce. They can also use letters and words – an activity that makes writing out and learning spellings much more interesting!

Puzzle time

"Pleasure, practice and purpose: the recipe for success provided you have time to think and try things out for yourself."

Improve visual perceptual skills, develop problem-solving behaviour, help pupils learn about strategies and much more. This miracle activity is the jigsaw puzzle. It works like magic, provided that pupils talk about the shapes and the colours as they make the puzzle.

Taking it further

Make it more challenging by turning the puzzle pieces upside down before making the puzzle. There are no colour clues so pupils have to rely solely on the orientation of shapes. It is an excellent activity for practising the use of directional language. Make sure that pupils describe the piece they are looking for before they try any out. This encourages them to pay attention to the relative size of the 'holes' and 'bumps' and to select on the basis of logic rather than trial and error.

Solving a jigsaw puzzle gets pupils thinking and talking about the problem-solving process and the importance of organisation. In 1945, the mathematician George Pólya identified four principles of successful problem-solving behaviour: understand the problem; devise a plan; carry out the plan; look back at your work. Apply this approach to making a jigsaw puzzle. Asking questions is an essential part of understanding each step. What is the task? Do you have the pieces you need? How are the pieces the same or different? Can you sort the pieces out into similar groups? What strategy can you use? Can you select relevant pieces? Have you achieved your goal?

- Pupils do the puzzle without looking at the picture. They sort the pieces into two categories: straight sides and no straight sides.
- Pupils use the straight-sided pieces to make the outside edge of the puzzle. They find a corner piece and describe the shape of each side using simple words such as 'straight, bump and hole'. They discuss the colour and shape of the piece in the puzzle, and then describe the piece they need. They select possible pieces and try them (see online resource).
- When the outside edge is completed, they assemble the central portion using similar reasoning to identify pieces. Pupils are rewarded with a completed puzzle.

Classroom design

"The classroom makes my brain hurt. There are things all over the walls and hanging from the ceiling." (Carrie, aged 10)

Your classroom environment sends a strong message to your pupils. Make sure it is the message you intend.

Mathematics is about making sense of the world by seeking out pattern and order. Do your wall displays endorse this message? Does your classroom provide a sense of purpose and an example of organisation?

Ask a colleague to spend five minutes in your classroom and then feedback their feelings about the room and the key features they remember from the walls. Do the same for them. How could you improve your displays?

- Purpose – what is the purpose of the display? Display pupils' work to reward effort as well as excellence; to spark interest in the topic being taught; to provide useful information such as key words. Discard anything that is purely decorative; it is using up valuable wall space and distracting from what is relevant.
- Communication – is the display easy to read and understand? Use images and arrows judiciously to enhance understanding. Keep headings short and simple. Use an appropriate scale for text.
- Colours – do the colours reinforce the message or diminish it? Use bright colours sparingly. Pastel or neutral backdrops help to project the display. White space, or negative space help focus on the content.
- Layout – where is the focal point of the display? Too often items are scattered in a random array. Take tips on composition from artists: direct the eye with leading lines (as you do in flow charts); use scale and hierarchy to draw attention to the most important item.

Teaching tip

Plan your classroom displays with the needs of pupils with visual perceptual difficulties in mind. A bold and busy jumble is distracting for all pupils but particularly for those who have difficulty maintaining focus.

Bonus idea ★

Calmer environments have been found to improve pupil behaviour and reduce stress.

Number toolkit

"Make sure you have the right tools for the job."

Every child should have a number toolkit. Concrete materials put the focus on understanding, rather than merely reproducing procedures.

Teaching tip

Look for base 10 equipment in which the tens rods and hundred squares have smooth surfaces. Some manufacturers produce them demarcated into ones, which obscures the message of the principle of exchange (see Idea 53). Pupils need to interpret the larger group as a whole quantity rather than a collection of ones.

It is vital to have plenty of suitable equipment for pupils to use and explore themselves. During the process we call thinking, new concepts are linked to information already stored in the brain. The more perceptual senses a pupil uses, the more areas of the brain are involved and the stronger the memory that results. This is why multi-sensory teaching is so effective: pupils speak, touch, see and hear while they model and draw and write.

A basic number toolkit contains the following (illustrated version available online):

- base 10 equipment (Dienes blocks)

- bead strings

- packs of cards, e.g. numerals; dot patterns

| 1–10 Pattern cards | 0–10 Number cards | 11–20 Number cards |

- counters or other small objects the same size and colour, e.g. plastic or glass nuggets

- Cuisenaire rods

- dice, including 1–3, conventional 1–6 and
  10-sided dice numbered 0 to 9 and 1 to 10

- pencil, paper (squared and plain) and
  coloured pencils to match the Cuisenaire rod
  colours

- ruler – use metric rulers with the whole
  numbers marked at the lines rather than
  showing the numbers in the space between
  the intervals as these cause confusion
  between the concepts of counting numbers
  and measuring numbers (see Idea 59).

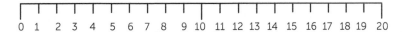

Numbers to 10

Part 2

IDEA 14

How many are there?

"Counting is much more than saying the number words in order."

Counting answers the questions: 'How many are there?' (cardinal value) and 'Which position is it in?' (ordinal aspect).

Teaching tip

The pronouns 'I' and 'you' are difficult for some pupils to understand because the meaning depends on who is speaking. Solve the problem by using names.

Pupils learn to count by moving objects and synchronising with each number word. They need to practise counting small quantities (see also Idea 3) and be able to compare the size of quantities using comparative terms such as 'more than', 'same as', 'less than'. This simple track game practises both of these, providing a strong visual image to make the concepts of 'more than', 'same as' and 'less than' clear.

- Each player has a 'caterpillar track' – a track consisting of ten circles in a line (see online resources) – and ten counters.
- Players take it in turns to roll a 1–3 dice and count out the quantity of counters indicated.
- They place the counters on their track. When pupils can confidently count to three, encourage them to count the counters onto their track.
- At the end of each turn, players say who has *more* counters. (Make sure pupils understand the concept of 'more than' and 'same as' before introducing the term 'less than'.)

Player A
Player B

- Player A says: 'I have more than Player B.'
  Player B says: 'Player A has more than me.'
- Players continue taking turns and adding counters onto their track. The winner is the first to reach the end of their track.

Taking it further

Do not rush. It takes an enormous amount of repetition for pupils to develop confidence in basic counting.

Dice patterns

"I get muddled up between 4 and 5. The dice patterns look the same to me."

The six-sided dice with its distinctive dot patterns (known as pips) has been in use for thousands of years – long before Arabic numerals. The patterns provide memorable, visually distinctive images, which provide the perfect foundation for building number knowledge.

Learn to count to six, and develop pattern recognition skills, by playing with dice. Pupils need plenty of practice and time to learn to recognise the dot patterns. Pupils with poor pattern recognition skills may need to repeatedly count the individual pips in each number pattern before they can recognise them. Let them count. It is in the act of counting and comparing the patterns that they figure out the relationship between numbers.

- Number bingo – each pupil writes the numbers 1 to 6 in a line. If they cannot write, then provide the row of numbers. Players take turns rolling a dice. They say how many dots there are, and cross out the correct number on their list. The winner is the first to cross out all six numbers.

- Order towers – each pupil has six dice. The aim of the game is to be the first to stack their dice on top of each other in a tower in strict numerical order, starting with the number one at the bottom. (Those who are less dexterous may prefer to build the sequence as a row instead.) All pupils play at the same time; they work independently but are racing against each other to complete their tower first. At the command to start, all players start rolling their dice. Once they roll a 1, they start building their tower. They continue until their tower is complete.

Teaching tip

Give pupils extra practice by playing board games such as ludo, where players roll a dice and move a counter along an unnumbered track so that the emphasis is on linking the number on the dice to the number counted. Avoid games with numbered tracks at this stage as they cause confusion.

Taking it further

Explore the history of dice and what they were used for. Dice first appeared more than 8,000 years ago. The first board games were played in Ur in Mesopotamia about 3,000 BC. The dice we use today – a cube with little dots – first appeared in Mesopotamia in 1,000 BC, long before the Arabic numerals we use.

Number components

"Big numbers have small numbers inside them."

Dice patterns make it clear that all quantities greater than one are made of smaller quantities. This activity helps pupils understand the relationship between a number and its components; knowledge that is essential for effective calculation.

Teaching tip

Pupils should show 2 and 3 with counters in a vertical or diagonal orientation rather than horizontally to help keep each pattern distinct from the one adjacent to it. Sometimes pupils put each of the patterns of 4, 5 and 6 in a single line. This indicates poor pattern recognition skills. They will need to do work on understanding pattern.

Bonus idea ★

Teach the concepts 'horizontal' and 'vertical' The teacher gives the instruction: 'Vertical.' Pupils stand up straight with their arms above their heads and shout: 'Vertical.' The teacher gives the instruction: 'Horizontal.' Pupils lie down stretched out on the floor and shout: 'Horizontal.' The teacher varies the calls and pupils respond as quickly as they can. Whoever is last to move into the correct position is out. Who will be the last person left?

Discuss the composition of the various dice patterns, drawing attention to the patterns within the patterns. Introduce the terms 'double' and 'half'.

- Pupils use counters to make the conventional dice patterns.

- Pupils then draw the dice patterns and write the numbers underneath them. Pupils with poor motor skills can use sticker dots.
- Model the patterns of 2 and 4 and discuss the relationship between them. Use the preposition 'of' rather than 'for' to emphasise that the model *is* the representation of the number, e.g. 'Look at the pattern of 2. Now look at the pattern of 4. I can see a 2 and a 2 inside the pattern of 4. Can you see that 4 is made of 2 and 2?' Pupils point to 2, then to 4 and indicate that 2 and 2 makes 4. Vary the language but keep sentences short and point to, or move, counters to reinforce the reasoning. Do not rush.
- Describe the relationship in other terms, always adjusting the model to make the meaning explicit, e.g. '4 take away 2 leaves 2.' Then: '4 is double 2, so, double 2 makes 4.' At a later stage introduce the concept of half: '2 is half of 4. Half of 4 is 2.'
- Pupils discuss the relationship between the patterns of 3 and 6 in the same way.

Three in a row

"Learning takes place when pupils are interested in what they are doing."

Reinforce the importance of one-to-one correspondence by playing traditional dots in a row games. This activity also hones focus and concentration.

This game requires pupils to quickly enumerate small quantities of objects and compare them. This ability is an essential numeracy skill and was discussed in Ideas 3 and 14. The task enhances visual discrimination skills as players need to isolate their relevant counters from all those on the board. Play 'Three in a row' then adapt the rules to play 'Four in a row' and 'Five in a row'.

Three in a row is a game for two players. The equipment consists of plenty of coloured counters and a game grid with large squares (2cm²) (see online resource.) Each player has their own colour of counters. Players take it in turns to place a counter in a square. New counters must be adjacent to an existing counter. The aim is to form a line of three counters. They can be oriented horizontally, diagonally or vertically. Players need to be aware of their opponent's moves so they can block them to stop them forming three in a row. The winner is the first person to achieve a line of three counters.

Teaching tip

Do not confuse 'Three in a row' with the game tic-tac-toe (also known as noughts and crosses), which is restricted to a 3 x 3 grid.

Bonus idea ★

You can play a pencil and paper version of this game as a quick filler activity using 1cm² paper (available online). Each player has a different coloured pencil. One player marks their moves using a coloured-in circle and the other player draws a cross.

Dot patterns: numbers to 10

"I like the dot patterns because I can see the number in my head and I can see what it is made of."

Dot patterns provide strong, visually distinct images of the numbers to 10. The key components of doubles and near doubles bonds are explicit in the patterns.

This activity builds on Idea 16. Pupils derive dot patterns for the numbers 7, 8, 9 and 10. Each pattern shows clearly that it is made from two of the dice patterns. First make the doubles patterns of 8 and 10 and then the near doubles patterns of 7 and 9.

Pupils begin by making the conventional dice patterns 1–6 using counters and revising the relationship between 2 and 4, and 3 and 6 (see Idea 16). Encourage them to use their own words.

- Making 8 – pupils make one pattern of 4 and another pattern of 4 below it. Make sure that the patterns of 4 are distinct within the larger pattern of 8. The impact is lost if they appear to be two lines of 4. Pupils talk about the relationship between 4 and 8, e.g.

- 'This is the pattern of 4. If I add 4 more counters I will have 8 counters.'

- 'This is the pattern of 8. I can see that 8 is made of 4 and 4. Double 4 makes 8. Half of 8 is 4.'

- Making 10 – derive the pattern of 10 using the pattern of 5, e.g.

- 'This is the pattern of 10. I can see that 10 is made of 5 and 5. Double 5 makes 10. Half of 10 is 5.'

A near doubles pattern is a pattern that is one more, or one less than a doubles pattern. Investigate both ways of making the near doubles. It is easiest to start with 8 and 10 and make the patterns that are one less.

- Making 7 – pupils talk about the relationship between 6, 7 and 8. They explain that 7 is between 6 and 8. They explain that 7 is 1 more than 6 and 1 less than 8. Start with the pattern of 8 to derive the pattern of 7, e.g.

- 'This is the pattern of 8. If I take away 1 counter, I will have 7 counters.'

- 'I can see that 7 is made of 4 and 3. I can move the counters to show the pattern of 4 and the pattern of 3. This is the pattern of 7.'

- Making 9 – pupils follow the same method to derive the pattern of 9 from the pattern of 10. Make the pattern of 10 and say, 'If I take away 1 counter, I will have 9 counters.'

- 'I can see that 9 is made of 5 and 4. This is the pattern of 9.'

Ask pupils to draw all the dot patterns on squared paper.

Taking it further

Allow pupils plenty of time to explore the relationships between a doubles number and its components. This knowledge will be applied to calculations with larger numbers. Being able to quickly ascertain half of a number is invaluable for working flexibly with number lines to help pupils locate numbers. (See Idea 69.)

Visualising dot patterns

"Recognising and remembering are different skills. Pupils need strong visual images which they can use for problem solving."

Visualisation is an efficient and flexible way of remembering complex information. Visual images reduce the load on working memory so help problem-solving. It is not enough to look at an image; pupils need to construct visual images through plenty of multi-sensory work. First they need to recognise patterns.

Teaching tip

If pupils draw the dots spaced too far apart, the impact of the cardinal value of the number is lost. It may also indicate that they have poor pattern recognition skills. Give them plenty of time and opportunity to draw the patterns on 1cm² squared paper.

Pupils develop visual discrimination skills by identifying distinctive features of the dot patterns. They need to associate the dot patterns with the correct number. These activities help pupils recognise, and then remember, the dot patterns – provided that they talk about what they are seeing and doing.

- Pattern hunt – each pupil has a pack of 1–10 dot pattern cards. Pupils pool the cards and scatter them face up on the table. Each player takes it in turns to roll a 1–10 dice. They find a card with the same pattern and place it, face up, in front of them in the correct sequence. If they already have the matching card, play passes immediately to the next player. The winner is the first person to have three consecutive cards in their row.
- Recalling dot patterns – put the cards away and ask the pupils to draw the dot patterns. They should pay attention to the spatial arrangement on the page, as well as clear and accurate configuration of dots. Each dot should be a reasonable size and coloured in. This makes the patterns clear. (See Idea 18)

The memory game

"Now I can see the dot patterns in my head and they help me to calculate."

Play a game to visualise the dot patterns and learn the key facts of doubles and near doubles as well as improving memory.

This game involves finding matching pairs of cards. It is an old stalwart aka 'Pairs' or 'Pelmanism'. In this version, pupils talk about the patterns on the cards and where they are on the table. This helps them learn key number facts as well as harnessing the tremendous power of the game to improve memory, concentration and logical reasoning skills.

- You will need one set of number cards 1–10 and one set of dot pattern cards 1–10. Each set should be a different colour. Shuffle the cards and place them face down on the table in a structured arrangement. This helps pupils with poor spatial skills access the game.
- Players take turns to turn up a number card and then hope to turn up the matching dot pattern card. For maximum learning, pupils explain what they are doing, e.g. player turns up 7 and says: 'I have 7. I am looking for the pattern of 7 which is made of 4 and 3.'
- If they select the matching card, the player keeps the card and has another turn. If not, the player talks about what they see, e.g. 'I needed 7. I turned up the pattern of 5.'
- After several rounds, add another layer of thinking skills: each player begins their turn by identifying some of the cards on the table (without pointing to them) *before* they turn any over. This lays the foundations for selecting the best strategy. Pupils can choose to turn up a pattern card first.
- The winner is the player with the most cards when they have all been paired up.

Teaching tip

Before the game starts, ask pupils to check that all the cards are there by putting them out in sequence and matching them up. This gives additional practice in sequencing.

Taking it further

Practise number bonds by using a set of cards with the doubles and near doubles bonds:
1+1, 1+2, 2+2, 2+3, 3+3, 3+4, 4+4, 4+5, 5+5 (see online resources).

Shut the box

"A simple and straightforward way to learn what the symbols mean."

Map numerals to dot patterns by playing the old favourite, 'Shut the box'. It allows less confident pupils time to think, and count the dots if they need to.

First play 'Shut the box', then play 'Open the box'. You will need a 1–10 dice and one set of dot pattern cards (1–10) for each player.

Shut the box

Players shuffle their cards and put them in a line, face up in order. Players take turns to roll the dice and turn over the card with the same value, e.g.

Player A has rolled 5 and turned over the pattern of 5.

If a player has already turned over the matching card, that is the end of their turn. The winner is the first player to 'shut the box' by turning over all their cards.

Open the box

Leave all cards in the final position from the end of 'Shut the box' (to give the losing player a head start) and play the game in reverse: players take turns to roll the dice and turn *up* the card with the same value. The player who lost 'Shut the box' starts. The winner is the first player to 'open the box' by displaying all their cards.

Writing numbers

"I keep muddling up 2 and 5, and also 6 and 9. Sometimes 3 looks like E."

Take time to teach pupils to form numbers correctly. Untidy and incorrect numbers lead to calculation errors – especially when the idiosyncrasies persist into adulthood!

Reversing digits is a common problem. All digits apart from 0, 1 and 8 can be reversed. Young children often reverse letters and digits when they are learning to write; however continued reversals may be a sign of visuospatial difficulties.

Teach number writing as a handwriting exercise so children can think exclusively about the number formation (see online resource). Teach a simple, clear script so that each number is distinct. Write 'one' as a single vertical stroke without a 'hook' to avoid confusion with seven.

Pupils use a ruler to draw a vertical line on the page. They then write each number to the right of the line as demonstrated in the diagram on the right, starting at the left hand edge of the page (with the exception of the number 9). All digits start from the top. They should use a different coloured pencil for each number.

- Guess my number – Player A stands at the whiteboard ready to write, and Player B uses their finger to write a digit on Player A's back. It is important to use the whole arm movement to make it a reasonably large size. Player A writes on the whiteboard, trying to reproduce the lines that they feel. Interpreting the feeling helps recall the correct orientation of the digit.

Teaching tip

Good handwriting starts with good posture and correct pencil grip. Teach pupils to make fluid pencil movements before expecting them to write numbers or letters.

The estimation game to 10

"This is the best game for practising counting and getting a 'feel' for numbers."

Estimation is the ability to know roughly how many there are in a group of objects. It is crucial for working with numbers.

This game helps pupils to develop their skills in estimating by looking at a quantity and guessing roughly how many objects there are, then checking the estimate by counting. In any one game, objects should be a similar size.

- Each player draws up a score sheet to record their estimates.
- Scatter a handful of objects (10 or less) on the table. Allow players to look at them for a few seconds (not long enough to count them). Then cover them with a sheet of paper.
- Each player says how many objects they think there are. Everyone records all the estimates on their score sheet.
- One player counts the objects aloud and places them neatly in a single horizontal line.
- The winner is the player whose estimate is closest to the actual number of objects.

	Player A	Player B	Actual Number	Winner
Round 1	6	9	8	Player B

Tracking

"Accuracy is more important than speed."

Tracking is the art of searching systematically for relevant information. In this idea, the pupils use tracking to develop the skill of quickly recognising the dot pattern of each number.

Selecting relevant information from a mass of data is an important learning skill. Give pupils a sheet containing a variety of dot patterns (available online). Ask them to track line by line to find the pattern of a particular number.

Pupils work from left to right and use a pencil to draw a line underneath the row of patterns as they work. When they reach each target pattern, they continue under the item and circle it using an anti-clockwise movement (see below) before returning to the track below the target pattern. When they have finished, pupils go back and carefully check each line for errors.

Can pupils improve? Set a benchmark score. Record the time taken to finish the sheet and check it. Record the number of errors. Track for a different number each day, then do the same tracking sheet again in two weeks' time and compare the score with the initial attempt.

Taking it further

When pupils are tracking, the tip of the pencil helps them focus their eyes and their attention. This tracking activity also works well for developing quick recognition of the pairs of numbers that make 10.

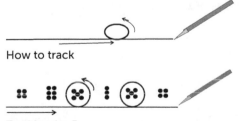

How to track

Tracking for 5

Calculation: doubles and near doubles

"I hear and I forget. I see and I remember. I do and I understand."
Confucius (circa 500 BC)

The dot patterns make it easy to learn the key number facts — the doubles and near doubles bonds. Show dot patterns in triad formation to make the relationship between addition and subtraction clear and write equations.

Provide a template for pupils who have difficulty drawing the triads and arranging them on the page (available online).

At this stage omit the equation in the form $1 = 2 - 1$ as pupils find it conceptually too difficult to follow.

Use the word 'split' rather than 'divide' which has connotations of equal parts.

It is important not to use addition or subtraction signs on the triad diagram or the symbolic representation. This obscures the conceptual relationship. Sometimes people join the lower two numbers to form a triangle. Again this obscures the relationship between the number and its components.

A triad is a diagram that clearly shows how a number can be split into two components which may, or may not be equal. In this activity, pupils use counters to model numbers on a triad base sheet (see online resource). Pupils move the counters as they explore the structure within each number. Record the information as diagrams and equations.

- Model the pattern of 2 in the top oval on a triad mat and say: 'This is the pattern of 2.'
- Move one counter into each of the lower ovals whilst saying: 'I split 2 into 1 and 1.'
- Draw a diagram and write what the triad represents. Start with $2 = 1 + 1$ as this relates directly to the description '2 is made of 1 and 1'.

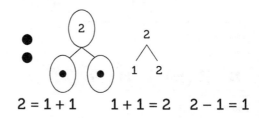

$$2 = 1 + 1 \qquad 1 + 1 = 2 \qquad 2 - 1 = 1$$

Pupils work in pairs to investigate how each number from 3 to 10 can be split into their doubles and near doubles components.

Taking it further

Take time to work with small numbers to ensure that pupils grasp the triad concept securely. Pupils can then generalise this knowledge when partitioning multi-digit numbers.

- Each pupil has 10 counters, a triad base sheet and a recording sheet.
- Pupils take turns to model each number and spit it into its components.
- Both pupils record the information and the equations on their own recording sheet. See examples for 3,4, 5 and 6 below.
- It is important that they discuss what they are doing in their own words and that they read each equation using varied language (see Idea 29).

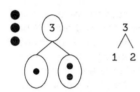

3 = 1 + 2   1 + 2 = 3   3 − 1 = 2
3 = 2 + 1   2 + 1 = 3   3 − 2 = 1

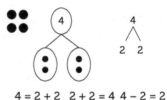

4 = 2 + 2   2 + 2 = 4   4 − 2 = 2

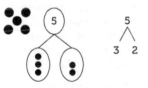

5 = 3 + 2   3 + 2 = 5   5 − 3 = 2
5 = 2 + 3   2 + 3 = 5   5 − 2 = 3

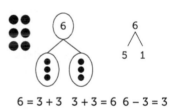

6 = 3 + 3   3 + 3 = 6   6 − 3 = 3

Get them questioning

"Too often teaching focuses on getting the right answer. Problem-solving requires asking the right questions."

Very young children have a seemingly inexhaustible supply of questions. Too soon this habit of curiosity is extinguished. They believe that only the right answer matters; the one in the teacher's head. Rekindle their enthusiasm by prizing the problem-solving process as much as the result.

Teaching tip

For a shorter game, introduce a rule that the object in question can be seen in the classroom. This also helps to keep everyone paying attention as they scan the room for clues.

The problem-solving process involves asking questions: 'What do I want to find out?' 'What information do I have?' 'How can I summarise it in a diagram?' Talking, looking, modelling and applying previous knowledge are all part of the thinking process. Too often that initial spark, the question, is overlooked. Hone questioning skills by playing the word game '20 questions' in which pupils have to think of apt questions.

This game is suitable for two players or for the whole class. One player is the answerer and all the others are the questioners. The answerer thinks of something and the other players are allowed up to 20 questions to discover what it is.

- The answerer thinks of something, writes it on a piece of paper and hands it to the teacher. (This prevents arguments later.)
- The answerer states whether they are thinking of a person, a place or a thing.
- The questioners take it in turns to ask one question each to which the answerer can only answer 'yes', 'no' or 'I don't know'.
- The teacher keeps a tally of the number of questions asked on the board.
- Can the questioners solve the mystery before the question quota runs out?

Taking it further

Once pupils can work with numbers up to 100, play 20 questions to identify a target number.

Bonds of 10

Part 3

Caterpillar tracks

"Understanding 10 is the bedrock of numeracy."

In this game, pupils learn to add on small quantities. This game is played on a track, which helps pupils develop a feel for the quantities and their relationships to 10. The track provides a strong linear image of 10, which is the foundation of the base 10 number system.

This game builds on Idea 14. Players take turns to roll a dice and place counters on their caterpillar track (see online resources).

- The player takes the specified number of counters and places them above the circles on the track. Then they count them as they move the counters into position.

- On each subsequent turn, the player puts the counters above the circles. They say how many counters are on the track, and then 'count on' as they place the new counters in position, e.g. Player A rolls 3 and counts out 3 counters which are placed above the track as shown. Then Player A says: 'I have two', referring to the number on the track and then continues, 'three, four, five' as the new counters are added on.

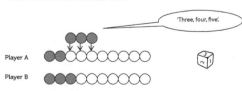

'Three, four, five.'

- The winner is the first player to reach the end of their track.

Fun beads

"Moving beads on a string is enjoyable and has a calming effect."

Use a string of ten beads to practise the bonds of 10.

This activity provides strong visual and kinaesthetic feedback to help instil the bonds of 10. Moving beads on a string also reduces stress – something that has been known for thousands of years and is still in use today.

The ten-bead string consists of five beads of one colour and five beads of another. This emphasises the key double fact of 5 + 5 = 10. The beads are threaded in a special way so that they stay in position once they have been moved.

Encourage each pupil to make their own bead string (see online resource).

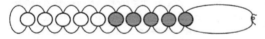

Ask pupils to show a specified number of beads and then say how many are covered up in their hand. Then pupils say how many they have altogether, e.g.

Teacher says: 'Show me 6. How many are hidden in your hand?'

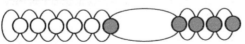

Pupils each display 6 beads and reply: 'Four in my hand.' Then they uncover all the beads and say: '6 and 4 makes 10.'

Bonds of 10 triads

"You mean I only have to learn six facts?" Adam, aged 8.

How many different ways can you split 10 into two numbers? Pupils explore the ways in which two numbers can be combined to make 10.

Addition is commutative (a + b = b + a) so pupils only need to learn the six bonds of 10. These are: 5 + 5, 4 + 6, 3 + 7, 2 + 8, 1 + 9, 0 + 10. Triads make it clear that these facts can be expressed in a variety of ways. Each pupil will need a triad base sheet (online resource), ten counters and a sheet to record their findings.

Pupils work independently to find all the different bonds of 10. Encourage them to start with the doubles fact (5 + 5), which they should already know (see Idea 25).

- Each pupil draws the dot pattern of 10 at the top left of the sheet. Then they use counters to make the pattern of 10 in the top oval on their triad sheet. They say: 'I can split 10 into 5 and 5' as they demonstrate the meaning by moving the counters.

- They record their thinking in diagrammatic and numerical form as triads and underneath they write the equations that the triad represents. Pupils get maximum value from the activity by saying each equation as they write it.

10 = 5 + 5   5 + 5 = 10   10 − 5 = 5

- Do the same for all the bonds of 10.

Testing positive

"Learn to set a benchmark."

For many pupils, tests are a stressful, humiliating experience which confirm their feelings of failure. Use benchmark testing to set goals and show how regular testing can be used in a positive way to help them learn the bonds of 10.

Give pupils an assessment test (available online, or produce your own). Explain the purpose of the test is to find a starting point, or benchmark, so the pupils can find out if they improve with practice. Make it clear that they should do their best but they will not be graded on the results.

Pupils have two minutes to answer as many questions as they can. There are 30 questions covering key facts in various representations – addition, subtraction, missing number.

Do not mark the test in class! Discuss the results with pupils individually. Use the DARE model to set targets to help pupils improve their personal score with practice:

- **D**ecide: How many more questions will I be able to answer? (Suggest 5 more questions.)
- **A**ct: What activities can I do to learn to recall the bonds of 10 quickly? (e.g. model bonds using counters at least once a week.)
- **R**evise: How long will I spend revising the bonds of 10 each day? Which days do I plan to revise? (Draw up a timetable.)
- **E**valuate: When will I take the test again? (Suggest 3 weeks.)

Repeat the same test after the decided time. Discuss the results with each pupil individually, comparing with their previous attempt. Emphasise that improvements made are down to their own hard work.

> **Teaching tip**
>
> The target for improvement should be achievable so that pupils get the feeling of satisfaction that arises from doing better than expected. Always keep the tests to refer back to later. Repeat the process until pupils are confident about the bonds of 10.

> **Bonus Idea**
>
> The DARE procedure is a way of encouraging pupils to develop a positive feedback loop. You measure to find the starting point; set a realistic target for improvement; act to improve your knowledge or skill; and then evaluate it again. The pleasure derived from success is a great motivator to further effort in many areas of life.

Clear the deck

"The two numbers that make 10 jump out at me."

Recognising pairs of numbers that make 10 is essential for efficient calculation. This simple card game gives pupils practice without the pressure of competition.

Taking it further

Build on the idea of setting a benchmark (Idea 30). Suggest pupils use a stopwatch to check how long it takes to play one game. Keep a record of the time. Play the game once a day for a week. Then, time playing the game again. How long does it take to find all the pairs? Compare the time to the initial session. Have they got quicker?

- You will need two sets of number cards 1–10. Shuffle the cards. Place 12 cards face up in a 3 x 4 array. Place the remaining cards face down in a stockpile.

3	9	4	3	
1	6	5	7	Stockpile
2	5	9	8	

- Ask pupils to find two cards that add together to make 10. Remove them from the display. Continue to look for pairs of cards that make 10.
- When there are no more pairs, take cards from the stockpile to replace the cards that have been used. The activity ends when all the cards have been used.

Ten in a bed

"Putting the bonds of 10 to bed is much more fun than just writing them out."

Pupils find pairs of numbers that make 10 and put them onto their own specially designed bed.

Ten in a bed is a traditional game, which appears to have gone out of fashion. However it usually receives an enthusiastic response from young pupils. Make it personal by asking pupils to make their own bed for the game from an A5 piece of card. Recycle cardboard to make a thick bed that can be coloured or painted with their own designs.

You will need a bed base for each player and four sets of number cards 1– 9.

- Shuffle all the cards and spread them face down on the table.
- Each player takes four cards.
- Collect the remaining cards into a stockpile and place them face down on the table.
- Players look at their cards. If they have two cards that make 10 they place them on their own bed and replenish the cards they have used from the stockpile.
- If a player cannot make 10, they put two cards at the bottom of the stockpile and take two more from the top of the pile.
- Play continues until all the cards in the stockpile have been used.
- The winner is the player with the most pairs of cards.

> **Bonus Idea** ★
>
> Sing the traditional nursery rhyme, *Ten in the bed* (lyrics available online) to practise counting back from ten. Each pupil has a caterpillar track (see Idea 27) and puts ten counters on it. They remove one counter at each appropriate moment in the song. When there is only one left 'in the bed', the words change to: 'There was one in the bed, And the little one said: I'm lonely!'

The memory game: bonds of 10

"The most effective learning takes place when pupils are interested in what they are doing."

In this idea, the pupils learn the bonds of 10, improve memory skills and understand the relationship between addition and subtraction. Not bad for one game!

The memory game (Idea 20) is one of the most powerful learning tools there is – provided discussion forms part of the game. Develop flexible thinking by using cards with different representations of the bonds of 10. Pupils check they have all the correct cards first by matching them up appropriately. Then shuffle the cards and put them face down in an array.

- **Addition** – play with two packs of number cards 1–9. Players take turns to turn one card face up, read the number and say what number is required to make 10 then turn up another card. If it is correct, they say the bond e.g. '6 and 4 makes 10' and keep the pair of cards. If it is the wrong card, they replace it in exactly the same position. Speaking aloud helps them learn facts and improves reasoning skills.
- **Missing addend** – play with one pack of number cards 1–9 and one pack of missing addend cards. Each pack is a different colour. Players take turns to turn up a missing addend card and read it aloud using the word 'what' for the missing number. They then answer the question, e.g. $4 + ? = 10$. Player says: '4 and what makes 10? 4 and 6 equals 10. So I am looking for 6.' They then turn up an answer card. If it is correct, they keep the pair of cards. If not, they replace it in exactly the same position.

Subtraction tally game

"Tally success in subtraction."

Practise subtracting from 10 and learn to use a tally chart.

Pupils need to be able to quickly subtract a number from 10. This ability is crucial for effective calculation using the bridging-through-10 strategy with larger numbers. This game allows each pupil the time to think if they need it.

The game requires a pencil and paper for each player and a 0–9 dice.

- Players each draw up a tally chart with the numbers 1 to 10 in the left hand column and a column on the right for each player with space to record the tally.
- Players take turns to roll the dice and subtract the number from 10. It is essential that players say the calculation on each turn, e.g. Player A rolls a 6 and says: '10 take away 6 is 4.'
- All players record the answer on their tally chart.

Teaching tip

If a pupil has great difficulty, encourage them to use counters to make the dot pattern of ten and then subtract the relevant quantity to find the answer. This will strengthen the visual image of what subtraction means.

	Player A	Player B
1		
2		
3		
4	I	
5		
6		
7		
8		
9		
10		

- The winner is the first player to achieve a tally mark against each number.

A message to you

"There is enormous pleasure to be derived from puzzling things out."

Apply basic number bonds to crack the code and read the mystery message.

Taking it further

Encourage pupils to encode their own messages. If they find these letters restrictive, suggest they use different letters. The secret is to start with a word or message that uses ten letters or less.

Print out copies of the worksheet (available online). Pupils solve the equations to find out which letter belongs to each number. Each letter in these equations represents a different digit.

- Use number facts to 10, logic and reasoning to turn the letters into numbers.
- Write each letter below the matching number in the grid.
- Then decode the numbers to solve the mystery message: 8254 2 37429 621.

Write the equations in numbers.

$V + V = YM$ ....
$V - Y = E$ ....
$E + E = H$ ....
$Y + H = T$ ....
$H - R = Y$ ....
$E + G = R$ ....
$G + G = D$ ....
$YM = H + A$ ....
$A + A = E$ ....

0	1	2	3	4	5	6	7	8	9

A minute or few

"I don't have time to practise."

Help pupils practise their number bonds daily by including two dice ideas in the general classroom routine.

Give register-taking a number twist. Pupils say a bond of 10 instead of replying 'good morning' when their name is called.

- Appoint a daily dice monitor whose job is to roll a 0–9 dice and generate a list of numbers in random order. There will be one number for each person in the class. The list of numbers is written in columns on the board before school starts.
- As the teacher calls each name on the register, the dice monitor points to a number on the board and the pupil uses the number in a sentence that makes 10, e.g. the dice monitor points to 8; the pupil responds: '8 and 2 makes 10'; the dice monitor crosses out each number in the list as it is used.

Use the lull at the end of a lesson to play dice. Pupils work in pairs. They compete to say a bond of 10 or demonstrate it on a bead string.

- Player A rolls a 0–9 dice. Player B makes the number on their 10-bead string as quickly as possible. Can Player B show the bond on the bead string before the Player A says the bond of 10 in a sentence?

Player A rolls a 6. Player A says: '6 and 4 makes 10.' Player B splits the beads on the string into 6 and 4.

IDEA 37

All the number bonds

"There aren't many more to learn!"

Too often teachers and pupils want to hurry on to larger numbers. Don't! Understanding the internal structure of the numbers to 10 and the relationships between them is crucial to becoming numerate.

Teaching tip

Pay attention to the way that information is displayed on the page. By now pupils should be able to lay out triads and write the equations in a balanced way on the page. Provide a template for pupils who have difficulty drawing the triads and arranging them on the page (available online).

Pupils used triads and equations to learn the doubles and near doubles bonds in Idea 25. Then they learned the bonds of 10 (Idea 29). They can reason to derive the remaining number facts for the numbers to 10, however it is helpful to know all the other number bonds of the numbers to 10.

- Record all the addition facts for numbers to 10 in a chart (see below). Addition is commutative (a + b = b + a) so only one version of each fact needs to be recorded.
- Highlight the bonds that are already known: doubles and near doubles bonds, and bonds of 10.
- Discuss the remaining facts that need to be learned. Most of them involve adding 1 or 2.

2	1 + 1 = 2			
3	2 + 1 = 3			
4	3 + 1 = 4	2 + 2 = 4		
5	4 + 1 = 5	3 + 2 = 5		
6	5 + 1 = 6	4 + 2 = 6	3 + 3 = 6	
7	6 + 1 = 7	5 + 2 = 7	4 + 3 = 7	
8	7 + 1 = 8	6 + 2 = 8	5 + 3 = 8	4 + 4 = 8
9	8 + 1 = 9	7 + 2 = 9	6 + 3 = 9	5 + 4 = 9
10	9 + 1 = 10	8 + 2 = 10	7 + 3 = 10	6 + 4 = 10	5 + 5 = 10

- Use triads and equations to represent all the
  bonds for the numbers from 2 to 10. e.g.
  Diagrams of 8 and 9.

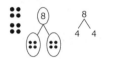

8 = 4+4   4+4 = 8   8−4 = 4

8 = 5+3   5+3 = 8   8−5 = 3
8 = 3+5   3+5 = 8   8−3 = 5

8 = 6+2   6+2 = 8   8−6 = 2
8 = 2+6   2+6 = 8   8−2 = 6

8 = 7+1   7+1 = 8   8−7 = 1
8 = 1+7   1+7 = 8   8−1 = 7

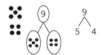

9 = 5+4   5+4 = 9   9−5 = 4
9 = 4+5   4+5 = 9   9−4 = 5

9 = 6+3   6+3 = 9   9−6 = 3
9 = 3+6   3+6 = 9   9−5 = 6

9 = 7+2   7+2 = 9   9−7 = 2
9 = 2+7   2+7 = 9   9−2 = 7

9 = 8+1   8+1 = 9   9−8 = 1
9 = 1+8   1+8 = 9   9−5 = 8

Slow snap

"I hate snap. I never have time to work out what is on the cards."

Slow snap gives pupils a chance to improve working memory as they practise number bonds.

Traditional snap is a nightmare for pupils who process information slowly. The emphasis on speed induces anxiety in weaker players and inhibits learning. In 'slow snap', players talk about the cards as part of their turn. This encourages pupils to look at the cards and process the information. The aim of the game is to match two cards that make 10.

- Shuffle four sets of number cards 1–9. Deal the cards equally amongst the players. Players keep their cards face down in a stockpile in front of them.
- Players take turns to turn up one card from their stockpile and place it face up on a new pile alongside so it is clearly visible to all players. They then read the number on the card and say which number they need to make 10.
- When two cards total 10, the first player to shout 'Ten snap' wins the round. The winner then says the winning bond and picks up all the cards in the winning, face up pile on the table to add to the bottom of their own stockpile.
- The game ends when one player has all the cards.

Question the question

"The brain is primed for questions. It learns and remembers better that way."

Empower pupils to think for themselves by encouraging them to ask questions to solve word problems.

Word problems put numbers in context. Make them a feature of every lesson. Set a few questions and ask pupils to make up their own.

Write a word problem on the board, e.g.

There are 5 passengers on a boat. The boat stops at the jetty to let 3 passengers off and 7 get on. How many passengers are on the boat altogether?

Pupils work in pairs to write down a series of questions to understand and analyse the problem. Pairs share their questions with the class. The teacher writes a selection of the questions on the board for class discussion. Classify the questions into categories.

- **Understand the question:** What do I want to find out?
- **Devise a plan:** What do I know? How many people are on the boat? How many get on and off? How can I summarise this?
- **Carry out the plan:** Can I use counters to model people? Can I draw a tally pictogram? How do I write the equation? Can I write the answer in a full sentence to make the meaning clear?
- **Look back**: What did I find out? Does the answer make sense?

There are no 'wrong' questions. If someone suggests an unexpected, or apparently unrelated question, find out why the pupil thought of it. Sometimes this leads to new ways of perceiving the problem.

> **Teaching tip**
>
> Pupils who use concrete materials to explore number relationships are already working with numbers in context. Using word problems puts numbers into other contexts: the real world of toys, sport, and food or the fantasy world of cartoons, wizards and spacecraft.

> **Bonus Idea** ★
>
> Important discoveries are often made by asking the 'wrong' question. In the 16th century, Copernicus challenged conventional thinking when he asked: 'What if the earth moves around the sun?' (Aristarchus of Samos had suggested the idea in the 3rd century BC but it didn't catch on.) Encourage pupils to find other examples of world-changing questions.

Cuisenaire rods

Part 4

Curious Cuisenaire

"The pupils love them. They are breathtakingly simple yet conceptually rich."

Cuisenaire rods are a powerful and versatile numeracy tool. They offer an engaging way to explore the key concepts of comparison and whole-part relationships, even before pupils can count.

Teaching tip

Encourage pupils to talk to each other about what they are doing. Comparative language is best developed in a meaningful context as happens in cooperative play.

Cuisenaire rods consist of ten rods of varying lengths, each with a distinctive colour. The basic unit is a 1cm^2 white cube. There are no markings on any of the rods and it is important that teachers do not assign numbers to each rod initially as the relationships are more important than the specific values. In time pupils will discover that the rods can represent the numbers from 1 to 10; later, they can be used to represent fractions.

Pupils need time to play with the Cuisenaire rods and build structures without adult interference. As pupils move the rods and talk about them, they discover underlying relationships that will eventually lead to concept formation. These ideas will be taught in a formal way later. Two key ideas are: comparison and whole-part relationships.

- **Comparison** – the rods vary in length. Special comparative relationships are emphasised by using colour values, e.g. the orange rod is double the length of the yellow rod.
- **Whole-part relationships** – the rods provide a visual image of the whole-part concept. By comparing rods and establishing that a particular length can be made of shorter rods, pupils discover that the whole can be split into parts. Conversely, two or more rods can be combined to make the same length as a longer rod.

Taking it further

Visit the Cambridge University NRICH website for a seemingly endless supply of free interactive activities using Cuisenaire rods. The page 'Cuisenaire Environment' is a good place to start (nrich.maths.org/4348).

Pattern analysis

"Human beings have a natural inclination to play and look for patterns. Give your pupils time to do so."

Analyse a design, then model it using Cuisenaire rods, draw it as a diagram and colour it in. This activity requires pupils to identify the component parts of a design.

Supply colour pictures of a design composed of Cuisenaire rods. (See online resource). It may represent something such as a dog or a flower, or be an abstract pattern.

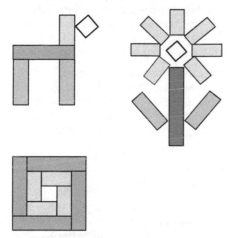

Pupils model the design using Cuisenaire rods.

They draw the design on 1cm² paper and colour it in. Initially pupils may need to place rods on the paper and draw around them. They will gradually find that it is easier to draw the rods by comparing the sizes and associating them with the number of squares on the paper. Encourage pupils to draw freehand and not to use a ruler.

Teaching tip

Print a variety of designs from the online resources on thick card so that they can be reused. Either deal cards out to pupils, or allow them to select a design. Alternatively, a design can be presented on the whiteboard. Whilst this appears to be easier from a preparation point of view, it may cause unexpected problems. Some aspects of visual perception are not fully developed in young children which makes it very difficult, if not impossible, for them to copy information from the whiteboard.

The key to patterns

"Analysis is a grown-up word for studying something carefully to work out how the parts in it fit together."

Use Cuisenaire rods to model a pattern, then extend the pattern into a sequence and explain each step of the process. This simple activity helps pupils learn to deliver and make sense of sequential instructions, which are fundamental for numerical reasoning.

Supply a picture of a simple pattern (see online examples). Pupils work in pairs. They work out what the basic elements of the repeated pattern are, describe the pattern and model it with Cuisenaire rods. Keep it simple. Let pupils decide whether to use colour names, or terms of comparative size, e.g. small, medium, large.

Pupils repeat the pattern a few times, discussing what they intend to do as they select each new piece. They draw a diagram of the sequence and write a short description of it, including using positional language, e.g.

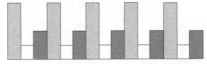

'The sequence begins with a purple rod. There is a small white rod next to it and after that is a red rod. I repeated this pattern.'

The more complex pattern below can be described in a variety of ways depending on how the pupil views the pattern, e.g. as two rows of green rods interspersed with columns of red rods with the white parts as either spaces or white 1cm^2 rods, or as a repeated T pattern.

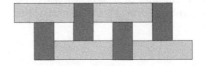

Secret sequences

"Talking unlocks the structure of the sequence."

Focus attention and improve speaking and listening skills by taking turns to describe a pattern and generate a sequence. This barrier game requires pupils to give coherent instructions and to carry out directional instructions.

Pupils work in pairs. They sit side by side and erect a barrier between them, e.g. a large open book, so neither can see the other one's model.

- Pupil A builds a simple sequence with Cuisenaire rods and describes it to pupil B (see Idea 42), e.g.

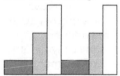

  'The pattern is made of rods. The rods are next to each other. The pattern is red, green, yellow, then red, green, yellow again.'

- Pupil B listens to the instructions and builds their interpretation of the pattern, e.g.

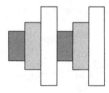

- Both pupils write a brief description of the pattern.
- Remove the barrier and compare the patterns. Are they the same? If they are not the same, how are they different? Are the rods horizontal or vertical? Do they align at the top or the bottom?

Teaching tip

Some pupils find giving clear instructions very difficult. They need to organise their thoughts and then convey them clearly. Remind them, 'Tell me what you see' (see Idea 9). This improves confidence as it makes it clear that they merely have to look at the objects and describe them. Make sure they start with simple sequences and gradually attempt more complex patterns. Slowly encourage the more complex language of direction, including horizontal and vertical.

Reflect on symmetry

"It looks exactly like it did in the mirror."

Give pupils Cuisenaire rods, squared paper and a small mirror for a happy half hour investigating symmetry.

Taking it further

Challenge pupils to create a shape with more than one line of symmetry. They can start with one symmetrical shape and then use reflective or rotational symmetry to create their new shape with more than one line of symmetry.

Recognising symmetry is fundamental to making sense of the world. A line of symmetry divides a symmetrical shape in half. Start from the other end and show pupils how to predict the result of 'flipping' a shape to construct a symmetrical shape.

Show pupils what is meant by a 'line of symmetry'. Hold up a symmetrical shape and fold it along the line of symmetry to prove that one half will fit exactly on the other. (Use a shape with only one line of symmetry at this stage.) Place a mirror on the line of symmetry, perpendicular to the page, to show that the reflection will be exactly the same size as the original.

Put a picture of five consecutive rods on the board as shown below. Pupils model the shape with rods and use their mirrors to predict what the symmetrical shape will look like. They make the shape and then draw and colour it.

Model ⟶   ⟵ Mirror image

Bonus Idea ★

Discuss the importance of symmetry in the natural world and how it is used to create balance and patterns in art.

Pupils construct their own models and draw them. They make the shape symmetrical by recreating a mirror image of the model. They use the mirror to check it is symmetrical.

The staircase game

"Learn to associate the numbers with the rods one by one."

Play the staircase game to familiarise pupils with the number assigned to each Cuisenaire rod and to practise the number sequence.

The sequence of Cuisenaire rods provides a strong visual image of the comparative size of numbers and makes it clear that each number in the sequence of natural numbers is one more or one less than the adjacent numbers. Pupils may already realise that each rod can represent a value from one to ten if they have drawn diagrams (see Ideas 40–44). If they are unsure which number to assign to each rod, they can work it out by measuring the rod with the white cube (one) during the game.

Each player needs a 1–10 dice and Cuisenaire rods. Players build their own staircases by placing rods in order of size from the smallest to the largest. (For a shorter game, the target is to collect four consecutive rods.)

Players take turns to roll the dice and select the matching rod which they place vertically in front them in the appropriate position. If a player rolls a number they have already got, play passes to the next player.

The winner is the first player to collect the sequence of ten rods.

> **Teaching tip**
>
> Encourage pupils to describe where each new rod will be placed, relative to the ones already in play. This gives them practice in positional language and makes them consider the relationships between numbers.

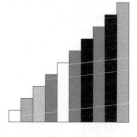

Pyramids and stairs

"Oh! The numbers go up in twos!"

Change the focus of the doubles numbers from the symmetrical model to the comparative size of the numbers by linking the pyramid model to the staircase model.

- Pupils create a pyramid to show the doubles numbers 2, 4, 6, 8, and 10.
- Pupils draw a diagram of the rod pyramid, colour it in and write the equations for each of the doubles facts alongside the relevant row, e.g.

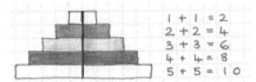

- The pupils move the rods on the model so they are all aligned on the left. This changes the arrangement from a pyramid design to a staircase image, e.g.

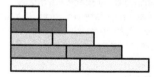

- Pupils draw the rod staircase in order to make it clear that although the facts are the same; the representation is slightly different.
- Discuss the difference in length between each row.

Double plus one

"I don't worry about forgetting number facts now I know how to figure them out."

Consecutive numbers differ by one. This activity reinforces recall of the doubles bonds and shows how to derive a new fact by adding one.

Discuss the relationship between adjacent numbers to emphasise that they vary by one. Pupils reason from a doubles bond to find the next number.

Use the interactive whiteboard to demonstrate the doubles pattern of 2. Point out that 2 is made of 1 and 1. Ask: 'What will 1 and 2 make?' Encourage pupils to reason that '1 and 1 makes 2, so 1 and 2 must be one more than 2. So 1 and 2 makes 3.' Demonstrate the 1 and 2 rods below the image of 1 and 1.

Pupils work in pairs to model each doubles bond and reason to derive the next number. They draw a diagram to illustrate each doubles number and the newly derived fact which will be a near-double number (see Idea 18). They write the equation for each row.

It helps to lay out and draw the Cuisenaire rods with the two rows related to each other adjacent and a small space left before tackling the next double number and its near double.

Teaching tip

Focus on teaching one concept at a time. Here the concept is that consecutive numbers vary by 1. Some teachers are tempted to teach the concept of odd and even at this stage because a doubles number is an even number and double plus one will always be an odd number. It is better to wait and teach odd and even as a separate concept later on (see Idea 62).

$1 + 1 = 2$
$1 + 2 = 3$

$2 + 2 = 4$
$2 + 3 = 5$

Number sandwiches

"It doesn't matter which order I add the numbers, the answer is always the same."

Use Cuisenaire rods to find out how many ways each number to 10 can be made of two other numbers.

A number 'sandwich' comprises two rods of equal length with the rods of the key components 'sandwiched' between them, e.g.

Demonstrate the number sandwich for 3 on the interactive whiteboard. To start with, include only one arrangement of rods for the filling and ask pupils to give you the other arrangement.

Pupils explore the numbers from 4 to 9. Encourage pupils to discuss what they are doing and compare their models with each other. Do they set them out in a systematic way? Does it matter if the rods are not arranged sequentially? Does it change the value if the rods are arranged in different ways?

Challenge pupils to find and explain a logical structure that can be generalised to other numbers, e.g. as one component increases by one, the other decreases by one.

Pupils draw a diagram to show all the components of each number and write equations next to each row, e.g.

3		
l	2	$1 + 2 = 3$
2	l	$2 + 1 = 3$
3		

Inside 10

"Whichever way you look at it, they add up to 10."

Establish a strong visual image of the components of 10 to consolidate these key facts.

Pupils build two 'staircases' from 1 to 10 using Cuisenaire rods. They carefully turn one model around so that if fits neatly onto the other one. The orange ten rods form the top and the bottom rows.

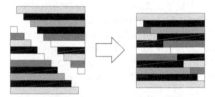

Pupils should draw a diagram of the model, but not colour it in (a base sheet is available online, if necessary). They write the numbers in each bar, then write the equations next to each row, e.g.

10		10
1	9	1 + 9 = 10
2	8	2 + 8 = 10
3	7	3 + 7 = 10
4	6	4 + 6 = 10
5	5	5 + 5 = 10
6	4	6 + 4 = 10
7	3	7 + 3 = 10
8	2	8 + 2 = 10
9	1	9 + 1 = 10
10		10

Bonus Idea ★

Make a large scale model of the Cuisenaire rods for a dramatic classroom display of the bonds of 10. Use recycled cardboard to make a 10cm x 10cm square and paint it white. This represents the number one. Give pupils a metre stick and ask them to make a rectangular bar that is 1 metre long and 10cm wide. This is 10, so paint it orange. Construct accurate bars for the numbers 2 to 9 and paint them in the Cuisenaire colours.

Make two sets of the rods and mount a display to show all the bonds of 10. This activity emphasises that the proportions stay the same even when the size is different.

Charting chatter

"Word problems are fun when you do them this way."

Use bar charts to illustrate information and make word problems easy to solve.

Bar charts are an essential part of summarising and comparing data in the modern world. Pupils need to understand how they are constructed in order to use them effectively. Cuisenaire rods provide the perfect model for bar charts. The pupil uses the rods to model information, and then draws a diagram. Hey presto! The result is a simple bar chart. They are particularly useful for solving comparison problems which involve finding the difference between two quantities, or making them equal.

Give pupils plenty of practice in solving problems and then ask them to make up their own questions. (See Idea 39).

- **Make them equal**, e.g. Sam scored 8 goals; Pat scored 3 goals. How many more goals does Pat need to score to equal Sam's score?

  | Sam | | 8 |
  | Pat | | 3 |

  Use either subtraction or missing addend.
  Subtraction: $8 - 3 = ?$ Missing addend: $3 + ? = 8$
  Answer: Pat needs to score 5 more goals.

- **Find the difference**, e.g. Ivan is 10 years old and Abi is 7 years old. What is the difference in their ages?

  | Ivan | | 10 |
  | Abi | | 7 |

  $10 - 7 = ?$ or $7 + ? = 10$
  Answer: The difference in their ages is 3 years.

Numbers to 20

Part 5

Taming the teens

"Avoid the turmoil caused by the 'teens' by patiently linking the spoken words to the numbers."

The 'teen' numbers cause particular problems for English speakers because the number words do not make the structure of the written number clear.

Pupils need plenty of practice saying the number words from 11 to 20 and counting objects, as well as seeing the written numbers. The term 'teen' numbers is used loosely to refer to numbers 11 to 19 even though eleven and twelve do not end in 'teen'. The suffix 'teen' meaning ten comes at the end of the spoken word whereas it is at the start of the written number, e.g. 14 is fourteen rather than ten-four. The number words from 11 to 13 create most difficulty because they bear little resemblance to the numbers one, two and three in the counting sequence.

- **Sequence numbers and names** – give pupils a set of word number cards eleven–twenty and ask them to make their own set of number cards 11 to 20. Pupils shuffle the cards and put them out in order, matching the numbers to the words. Make sure that pupils articulate the number words clearly, especially the endings 'teen' and 'ty'.
- **Cards and counters** – pupils take a number card between 11 and 20. They read out the number and take the correct number of counters. They count the counters into a line, leaving a small space after ten counters to make it clear that each 'teen' number represents '10 and some more'. They then remove the counters, take another card and model the number.

The 20 bead string

"I like moving the beads. It helps me understand the numbers."

Bead strings are a useful tool for working with and counting numbers, and emphasise the base 10 structure of the number system. Pupils need to be able to quickly locate the position of any number on the bead string through reasoning.

Pupils make their own bead strings to 20. They thread ten beads of one colour followed by ten of another colour on a cord and tie a knot at each end. The cord needs to be long enough to allow the beads to be moved on it whilst leaving space between the two groups of beads.

The teacher calls out a number. All the pupils locate the bead that represents that number on their string and hold up their bead strings to show the correct number of beads. They should move the beads so that there is a clear gap between the quantity required and the rest of the beads on the string.

Pupils take turns to describe how the targeted bead is related to the other numbers. Find as many different ways as possible to describe the relationships, e.g. 'Find bead 13.'

Possible responses include:

- 13 is three more than 10.
- 13 is between 12 and 14.
- 13 is one more than 12.
- 13 is one less than 14.

First past the post

"Now I see why ten ones is the same as one ten."

Use base 10 equipment to make it clear that one ten is worth the same as 10 ones. The game also introduces the idea of bridging through 10.

Teaching tip

The proportions of the base 10 cubes and rods reflect the idea that the two quantities are worth the same amount. Ensure that pupils can confidently model the principle of exchange in this way before introducing money. Monetary value is an abstract concept. The size of the coins bears no relationship to their relative value. This often causes confusion for pupils who have difficulty grasping the principle of exchange.

Understanding the principle of exchange is fundamental to working with the place value system. The principle of exchange is the idea that one item can represent a group of several smaller items.

- Each player has a track 20cm long with the 10cm point clearly marked (see online resource).
- Players take turns to roll a 1– 6 dice. They place the matching number of cubes on their own tracks.
- On subsequent turns, they count on as they put the cubes in position.
- When the count reaches the 10 marker, the players exchange 10 ones for 1 ten rod. It is important that the player places the ten rod next to the ones, as shown below, and describes the action as the rods are exchanged. This visuo-motor process, allied to speech, plays a central role in understanding the concept. When the exchange is complete, the player counts on any remaining cubes.
- The winner is the first person to finish.

Player had 5 and added 6.

'I exchange ten ones for one ten.'

'Ten and one is eleven.'

10 plus

"The teen numbers finally make sense when you make them like this!"

Understand that 'teen' numbers are composed of 10 plus a quantity between 1 and 9, and that 20 is composed of two tens. Relate the quantity to the written symbol.

Pupils model each number from 11 to 20 using base 10 equipment.

Pupils make a linear model, or rod 'train', using a 10 rod and some ones. They draw a diagram of the rods on plain paper. Seeing ten as a rectangular bar helps pupils focus on 10 as a quantity (the cardinal value) rather than a collection of ones. They draw the ones as individual squares.

Ask pupils to move the rods so that the 10 rod is vertical and the ones are arranged in the dot patterns. This shows the spatial representation of the number. They draw a diagram below their linear diagram and write a short description to explain that the number equals ten and some ones.

Teaching tip

Encourage pupils to use a variety of words to describe the ones, e.g. 'cubes' or 'blocks' which describes the objects, or the slightly more abstract 'units' or 'ones'. It is important that pupils start by using words that make sense to *them* and gradually refine their descriptions as they learn.

Taking it further

The spatial arrangement prepares pupils for formal place value work as it clearly shows a quantity of tens and the ones in the dot pattern. This representation will be used later to model standard written methods and make formal addition and subtraction much easier to understand (see Ideas 95 and 96).

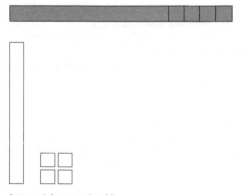

1 ten and 4 ones makes 14
10 + 4 = 14

Up the stairs

"The structure of the number system displayed for all to see."

Show how each 'teen' number is made of 10 and 'some more'. Make it clear that the numbers 1 to 10 are repeated within larger quantities. Harness the power of Cuisenaire rods for the wow factor and a lasting impact.

Model numbers

- Pupils work on their own, or in pairs, to make a rod staircase of the numbers to 10, building from left to right (see Idea 45).
- Discuss how to continue the pattern to make 11. Accept any suggestions and discuss why they may, or may not be appropriate. Guide pupils to adopt the 10 plus model.

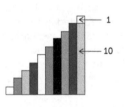 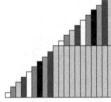

Bonus Idea ★

Construct a large-scale model of the numbers to 20 using discarded cardboard (see Bonus idea for Idea 49). One will be 10cm² and the 10 rod will measure 1 metre long. If there is a plentiful supply of cardboard, make a 3D model and stand the number up. This can be secured using plenty of sticky tape.

- It is very important that pupils talk about what they are going to do, and why, before they model each number. This helps the pupils to marshal their thoughts and focus on the elements of the pattern, rather than using the rods to mechanically expand the pattern.
- Encourage pupils to make the numbers in a vertical display as shown above. The impact of this arrangement appears to be greater than the horizontal orientation, though of course both are acceptable.

Bridging through 10

"Why do they call it bridging through ten? It should be make ten and add some more."

Bridging through 10 is the most important calculation strategy. It can be adapted to facilitate calculations with multiples of 10, or 100 and more. It is essential that pupils understand the strategy if they are to work effectively with number lines.

Pupils apply their knowledge of number components to a linear representation of Cuisenaire rods. This is an adaptation of the game 'First past the post' (Idea 53).

- Use a conventional 1–6 dice and a race board consisting of several 20cm tracks – one for each player – each with the 10cm point clearly marked with a thick line (see online resources).
- Players take turns to roll the dice and take the corresponding rod. On each subsequent turn, players put the new rod on the track, add the quantities together and exchange the two component rods for the resulting new rod.
- When play would cross the 10 marker, the player splits the quantity: they use some to make 10, and the remaining part is added on, e.g. in the diagram below, the player has 8 and rolls 5. They exchange the 5 for a 2 and a 3, in order to make 10+3=13.

Teaching tip

Use a 1–6 dice to reinforce the images of the dot patterns. Pupils derive greater benefit from this activity if they talk about what they are doing and predict the outcome of each turn before modelling it with Cuisenaire rods.

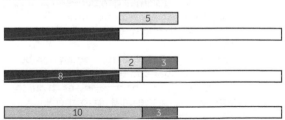

- The winner is the first person to reach the end of the track, or go beyond it.

Counting back

"Counting backwards is much more difficult than you think."

Use numbered cards and counters to teach pupils to count backwards.

Taking it further

Once pupils are able to count to 100, do the same exercise using a bead string instead of the counters.

Introduce counting backwards once pupils can confidently count forwards to 20. It is important to master this skill, as it is required for efficient calculation. Many pupils have difficulty counting backwards so use numbered cards to make it clear what counting back means. The cards also act as prompts.

Cards and counters

- Ask pupils to put out numbered cards from 1 to 10. They count forward pointing at each card and then they count back from 10 pointing to synchronise with each number word.
- Remove the cards and ask the pupils to count ten counters into a line. They point to each counter as they count back: *'Ten, nine, eight, seven . . . '.*
- Repeat the activity using cards to 20 and ten counters.

Back from any number

- Ask pupils to put out the sequence of cards to 20, leaving a small gap between 10 and 11.
- They turn all the cards face down.
- Choose a starting number and a number to end on.
- Ask pupils to point to the starting number, say the number and turn the card face up.
- Pupils then count back saying each number before turning the card up to check.
- They stop when the target number is reached.

Backtrack

"I like breaking up the tens."

Practise counting backwards and reinforce the principle of exchange as well as introducing the concept of decomposition.

The principle of exchange was introduced in Idea 53 when pupils exchanged 10 ones for 1 ten rod. Now they learn that 1 ten rod can be exchanged for 10 ones. This is called decomposition because the ten rod is 'broken' into ones. Some pupils have difficulty with the word decomposition so allow them to use 'exchange', or simply 'change'.

Teaching tip

It is essential that pupils talk about what they are doing as they make the exchanges.

In this game, pupils subtract quantities from 20. The equipment consists of a 1–6 dice and base 10 rods and ones cubes.

- Each player has a line of 2 ten rods to make 20, e.g.

- Players take turns to roll the dice to find how many to subtract.
- On the first turn, they need to exchange a ten rod for 10 ones. It is important that players show the decomposition by placing 10 ones above the ten rod and then exchanging them, e.g.

- The player subtracts by counting back, removing the designated number of cubes as they count.
- The winner is the first player to remove all their rods and cubes.

Taking it further

Practise mental maths skills by playing the same game using Cuisenaire rods. Pupils need to think about the number components before they choose which rods to take.

IDEA 59

Tracks and lines

"The difference between counting numbers and measuring numbers: difficult to explain, easy to see."

Play a game to highlight the difference between the numbers on a number track (counting numbers) and those on a number line (measuring numbers).

Teaching tip

Do not use + or − signs on the number line; these signs are sometimes used to indicate 'direction' on a number line, however this may cloud the understanding that the distance between two points is a fixed distance. It does not matter whether you start with the smaller number and add a quantity, or start with the larger number and subtract that same quantity, the distance will remain the same.

It is crucial that pupils understand how numbers are represented on a number line. It is a powerful tool that pupils can use to show calculations. More importantly, pupils need to understand number lines in order to interpret and use graphs.

There are important differences between the concepts of counting numbers and measuring number. Counting numbers are used to count quantities of distinct objects. They are shown on a number track that starts with the number 1. Each number occupies a separate space on the track.

Measuring numbers are shown at regular intervals on a number line. Each number corresponds to a point on the line, which shows how far it is from the start of the line at zero. All numbers, including fractions or decimals, can be shown on a number line. These continuous numbers are called measuring numbers because they are used to determine the size of continuous quantities such as distance, time and mass.

Play the game 'Hop and jump' to focus on the difference between counting numbers (displayed as a number track) and measuring numbers (recorded on a number line).

Hop and jump

In this game pupils move along a number track and a number line as they compete to be the first person to reach the end (available online). On the track, they count the number of circles they land on. The number line is different; here pupils count and mark each 'hop' as they move along the line from one point to another.

Use a 1–6 dice. Each player needs a numbered track from 1 to 20 and a number line showing the numbers from 0 to 20. Both of these are available online, although pupils should be encouraged to draw their own number line whenever possible.

- On each turn, the players take turns to roll a dice and move the number shown on both the number track and the number line.
- On their number track, they use one counter to 'hop' along the number track, counting aloud as they touch each circle, e.g. in the example below, the player finished their previous go on the number 13 and this go they have rolled a 5:

- On their number line, they use a pencil to draw the 'hops' as a series of arcs to move along their number line, and then they show the whole turn as a 'jump' – this is a single arc which encompasses the individual arcs from that turn. They write the number shown on the dice above the 'jump' arc, e.g.

- The winner is the first player to reach (or pass) 20.

Bonus Idea ★

Sometimes pupils want to add an extra circle at the beginning of the number track and label it zero. Do the following activity to show pupils why this is not necessary. Ask pupils to stand up and hop forward for three hops and count aloud as they do it. They will automatically count: 'One, two, three' as they hop. They do not say zero. In the same way they will count counters onto the numbered track saying: 'one, two, three' as the counter touches each number on the track. However on the number line, each hop is represented as an arc which shows the distance moved between one point and another.

The grid game

"The pupils were intrigued by the patterns of numbers that emerged."

Practise adding pairs of numbers up to 20 and introduce the idea of co-ordinates on a graph.

Teaching tip

In the early stages, encourage pupils to write the addition sum as an equation in the form a + b = c and b + a = c. This reinforces the commutative property of addition and helps them locate two different positions for the answer. However, only one answer square may be recorded on each turn.

- Give pupils a grid composed of 10 x 10 squares (available online). Each square needs to be big enough to write a two-digit number in it.
- Pupils number the rows 1 to 10 to the left of the vertical axis with 1 at the bottom and 10 at the top, and number the columns on the horizontal axis from 1 to 10.
- Each pupil has a different coloured pencil.
- Players take turns to roll two dice (numbered 1–10). They find the corresponding square using the numbers as co-ordinates. They add the two numbers together and write the answer in the square.
- The winner is the first person to get three in a row – horizontally, vertically or diagonally.

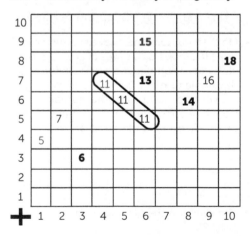

Addition tally game

"Juggling with facts to come up with new ones."

Apply key facts to derive bonds of 20 and record the answers in a tally chart.

It is important that pupils realise that knowledge of key facts can be generalised to any number, e.g. 3 + 7= 10 helps to work out 13 + 7, or 300 + 700. Pupils need to develop a flexible approach so start by practising the bonds of 20. If pupils struggle, ask them to model the bonds using Cuisenaire rods by extending Idea 56.

Addition tally game is a variation on Subtraction tally game (Idea 34). It allows each pupil the time to think if they need it. The game requires pencil and paper for each player and a 0–9 dice.

- Players each draw up a tally chart with the numbers 11 to 20 in the left hand column, and a column to record the tally for each player to the right.
- Players take turns to roll the dice and add the number required to make 20, e.g. Player A rolls a 2 and says: '2 and 18 makes 20.' The player puts a tally mark next to 18.

Taking it further

When pupils can confidently count to 100, play the same game with a different target number. Later they may like to play with numbers in the hundreds and thousands. This is good practice for working with calculations on number lines.

	Player A	Player B
11		
12		
13		
14		
15		
16		
17		
18	I	
19		
20		

- All players record the answer on their tally chart.
- It is essential that players say the calculation on each turn.
- The winner is the first player to achieve a tally mark against each number.

Odd and even search

"Isn't it odd that they didn't teach us like this in the beginning?"

Pupils use counters to explore the properties of odd and even numbers and develop a strong visual image that makes the meaning clear.

Teaching tip

Pupils may insist on splitting the quantity into two equal-sized groups because they have been taught that they 'have to do it this way'. Explain that this is not wrong. It is a perfectly acceptable way of demonstrating the concept. However, show them that it is easier to be certain whether a number is odd or even when the counters are put into twos.

Too often pupils learn 'odd' and 'even' as tags attached to specific numbers without understanding what the terms mean. The following simple investigation clarifies the meaning.

- Pupils can work in pairs. Both record all the numbers. The record sheet consists of two columns: one column is headed 'Even: Twos exactly' and the other is headed 'Odd: Twos with one left over'.
- Pupils scatter some counters. They put the counters into groups of two (with one on its own if necessary) but do not count them.
- Pupils explain in their own words, e.g. 'I put the counters into twos. There are none left over. The counters are exactly in twos. The number is even.'
- Pupils count the counters and write the number under the appropriate column.

Even Twos exactly	Odd Twos with one left over
8	

Pupils use their own words and phrasing to describe the meaning of each word and write the definitions. It is essential that the definitions use the language that the pupils are comfortable with, e.g. 'The number is even. I can put the counters into twos exactly.' Or: 'It is an odd number. I put the counters into twos and there was one left over.'

Numbers to 100

Part 6

Counting to 100

"Give pupils time to make mistakes. It is the only way they will learn to count with confidence."

Spend time exploring all the numbers to 100, especially those in the higher decades. Give pupils plenty of time to count real objects and organise them into groups of tens and ones.

Teaching tip

It is not necessary to build the spatial model for every number. Give pupils a list of numbers to model and make sure that they have plenty of practice with numbers in the higher decades.

In order to calculate efficiently, pupils need to have a feel for the quantity that two-digit numbers represent and be able to count fluently, yet they rarely have extensive practice counting larger quantities. Teachers assume that once they learn to count to about 30 or 40 they will understand the pattern and generalise it to higher numbers; often they cannot.

Use equipment to model numbers to 100. Start by counting to 30 and then gradually work through the numbers in each decade.

- **Linear counting** – use counters to model the numbers to 30. Each pupil puts out 20 counters leaving a small space between each group of 10. Ask them to add one more counter, and count from the beginning. Work through the sequence to 30, adding one more counter and recounting from the beginning each time. Pupils may realise it is easier to say the decade number for each group of ten rather than counting every counter, however some pupils take a long time to grasp this possibility. Give them plenty of time to consolidate their counting skills. Play the game '100 counter dash' (Idea 65).
- **Spatial representation** – use base 10 equipment to model each number in the sequence between 20 and 30 (see Idea 54). Pupils draw a diagram of each model and write the number in expanded form, e.g. 21 = 20 + 1 (two tens and one).

The 'teen' and 'ty' tangle ▷

"What is going on? I asked her to count in tens from 70 and she said: '80, 90, 20, 21.'!"

Emphasise the word endings and associate them with the written symbols to make a clear distinction between 'teen' numbers and decade numbers which end in 'ty'.

Pupils often confuse the 'teen' numbers 13 to 19 with the 'tens' numbers which are multiples of 10 and whose names end in 'ty' (see Idea 51). The confusion is apparent when pupils are asked to count in tens and they say, 'Eighty, ninety, twenty, twenty-one'. They clearly do not realise what the words mean and that the endings 'teen' and 'ty' have different meanings.

In this activity pupils practise reading numbers and categorising them according to the ending. Provide small blank cards and A4 paper.

- Pupils draw a table on A4 paper with two columns headed '-teen' and '-ty', and they make their own cards: they write the numbers 13 to 19 and the decade numbers 20 to 90 on one side of the pieces of card, and the corresponding number words on the back, highlighting the 'teen' and 'ty' endings.
- They shuffle all the number cards, then hold the pack with the number side up and read each number, emphasising the ending.
- Place the card under the correct heading on the base sheet, number side visible, e.g.

- When all the cards have been played the pupil turns the cards over and checks that they are in the correct column.

Teaching tip

Encourage pupils to prepare their own cards and base sheet as this helps focus their attention on the words. However, provide the equipment for pupils who have very poor handwriting. It is important that they see the numbers and the words written clearly as they read them (see online resource).

The 100 counter dash

"Wow! I didn't realise how big 100 is until I played this game."

Disguise counting practice as a race game. Give it a twist by reversing the direction on the roll of a dice so that pupils practise addition and subtraction.

Give pupils plenty of practice in counting out large amounts in order to develop a sense of the size of quantities. This activity also makes the comparative size of quantities clear.

Some pupils find counting backwards very difficult. This game helps build confidence because they can remove the relevant counters and then check their answer by counting from the beginning. It is a subtle way of linking subtraction and complementary addition.

Basic game: Count to 100

- Players take turns to roll a 1–10 dice and take the correct number of counters.
- They put the counters in a line, leaving a small gap between each group of 10 counters.
- Players say the total number of counters they have after each turn and check by counting.
- The winner is the first person to reach 100.

Backwards and forwards

- Each player takes 50 counters and puts them in a line, leaving a small gap between each group of 10 counters.
- Players take turns to roll a 1–10 dice and a dice marked + (add) and − (subtract).
- If the player rolls +, they add the designated number of counters to their line; if the player rolls −, they remove the designated number of counters from the line.
- The winner is the first person to reach 100.

Locate my number

"Where does one decade end and the next begin? The 100 bead string makes it clear."

Locate the position of a number by describing its position in relation to other numbers. This activity develops fluency in using comparative language.

Being able to quickly relate a number to other numbers in a sequence makes calculation much easier. This knowledge provides the foundation for understanding approximation and rounding.

Pupils work in pairs. Provide each pair with a 100 bead string, a pack of two-digit number cards and a pack of comparative word cards containing three sets of the words: 'between', 'more than', 'less than', 'before', 'after', 'next to' (see online resources).

- Pairs shuffle the word cards and place them face down in a pile. They shuffle the number cards and place them face down in another pile.
- Player A takes a number card and a comparative word card and keeps them hidden from Player B.
- Player A describes the position of the number using the comparative word on the card, e.g. Player A turns up the number 38 and the word 'next' and says: 'My number is next to 37. It is bigger than 37.'
- Player B says the number and finds the correct position on the bead string, then they have a turn.

Teaching tip

Focus on particular numbers by limiting the cards to choose from. The numbers at, and close to, the decade boundaries cause particular difficulty. Target numbers ending in 0, 1, 2, 8 and 9 as well as numbers higher than 50.

Digit swap

"My pupils were genuinely amazed to see how the position of the digits affected the size of the number."

Pupils build two-digit numbers to understand how the value of a digit depends on its position in a number. The model makes the relative size of numbers explicit.

Teaching tip

Focus on the higher numbers by using the number cards 4–9 only. Often pupils have experience using equipment with small numbers but do not do so with large numbers. The visual impact of 9 tens often surprises pupils.

Pupils model, draw and talk about numbers to make it clear what the digits actually mean in quantitative terms.

Pupils work in pairs. Provide each pair with base 10 equipment tens, rods and ones cubes and number cards from 2 to 9. Omit digit cards for 0 or 1 at this stage in order to focus attention on numbers larger than 20.

- Pupils shuffle the cards, then Pupil A takes two cards and puts them next to each other to form a two-digit number.
- Pupil A reads the number and models it using tens and ones.
- The pupils discuss the number and both draw a diagram of it. They write the number, explain how many tens and ones it is made of and write the equations to show what the number represents.
- The pupils leave the model on the table whilst Pupil B reverses the order of the two cards to make a different number.
- The pupils carry out the same routine as they did for the first number and then compare the first number with the second number.

Taking it further

Use the tally formation to model tens where appropriate. Show pupils that it is easier to model five by putting four rods vertically and the fifth diagonally across them. This is also called a 'gate check' as the image looks like a barred gate.

25

52

25 = 2 tens and 5 ones
25 = 20 + 5
20 + 5 = 25

52 = 5 tens and 2 ones
52 = 50 + 2
50 + 2 = 52

Card wars

"Spark an interest in place value."

Embed the concept of tens and ones in pupils' memory through frequent practice. Fill short spaces of time with this competitive place value game for 2–4 players.

The equipment consists of four sets of digit cards 1–9, a plentiful supply of base 10 tens and ones and a size card marked 'largest' on one side and 'smallest' on the other (available online).

- The dealer shuffles the cards and deals two cards, face down, to each player.
- All players look at their own cards but do not show anyone else.
- The dealer examines their own cards and decides whether the smallest or the largest number will win and turns the size card to show the appropriate word.
- All players put out their digit cards to make either the smallest or largest number they can, and they model the number using tens and ones (see Idea 67).
- Each player (starting with the dealer) reads their number in turn.
- The player with the largest/smallest number (as appropriate) says: 'I have the largest/smallest number.' They have won that round and so collect all the cards.
- The winner of the game is the player with the most cards when they have all been played.

Taking it further

Change the scoring system so that pupils keep a running total of their scores. This provides extra practice in the addition of multi-digit numbers. Decide before the game starts whether the smallest, or largest, total will be the winner.

Numbers on number lines

"Number lines are the linchpin of quantitative communication."

Master number lines by filling in missing numbers, reasoning to position numbers, and drawing number lines freehand.

Taking it further

Pupils who can happily place numbers on an empty line with reasonable accuracy are more likely to use them to help with calculation. Encourage pupils to use them whenever possible. Number lines provide a quick and easy way to find approximate answers, which are invaluable for checking work.

Number lines are everywhere in the modern world, from measuring distances to showing information on graphs and charts. The best way to develop confidence in using number lines is to spend time identifying and positioning numbers on empty number lines. Locating the midpoint on a number line, or relevant section of a number line, is a key concept to help establish the position of numbers.

- **Find mystery numbers** – give pupils practice in locating numbers on partially numbered lines, and then on empty number lines (see online resources). Encourage them to talk about the relationship between the numbers, e.g. 'Which tens numbers is it between?' 'Is it halfway between them?' 'Which number is it nearest to?' 'How close is it to that number?'

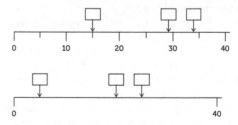

- **Reasoning to position numbers** – pupils sketch a number line from 0 (zero) to 40 and mark the numbers 10, 20, and 30 on it. They need to use reason to position the numbers using their knowledge of double and half.

Ask them to reason to position the following numbers on a new number line: 14, 25, 28, 32.

They work out where the numbers go by relating them to other points on the line and describing them in various ways such as: 'larger than', 'smaller than', 'before', 'after', 'between', 'midway between', 'nearer to'.

Example: pupil is asked to find 25. Encourage them to talk about the relationship between the numbers, e.g. 'Which decade numbers is 25 between?' 'How do I find the number at the midpoint? (Hint: I know that half of 4 is 2.) 'How can I find where 30 goes?' 'Which tens numbers is it between?' 'What is the midpoint between 20 and 40?' 'Where is the midpoint between 20 and 30?'

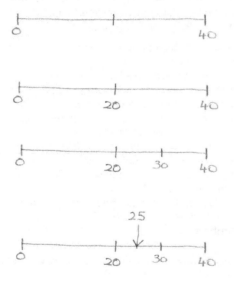

Bonus Idea ★

Try the free interactive number line activity at www.number-sense.co.uk. Pupils need to zoom in and out to adjust the scale of the number line in order to find the number they need. The game was developed as a research project at the London Knowledge Lab.

Zooming in

"I can't show the whole line on the page."

Number lines are an invaluable calculation tool. Use only the relevant part of the number line to make it easier to show the numbers. These are called partial number lines.

Many pupils with numeracy difficulties seem to find it really hard to draw a straight line freehand. Practise drawing straight lines in art lessons. Sketch random lines on a page to form shapes that can be coloured in. The final effect is a pleasing abstract work. Allow pupils to use a ruler if they find it very difficult to sketch a straight line.

Pupils are used to zooming in on computers to make information clearer. Use this idea to focus on the relevant section of a number line. Make it memorable by using an old-fashioned method – the magnifying glass.

- Pupils sketch a number line from zero (0) to 40 on A4 paper.
- Ask them to write in all the numbers from 17 to 32. They will find it very difficult as the numbers are too close together.
- Challenge them to use the magnifying glass to help find a way of making it easier.
- Ask them leading questions, e.g. 'Do you have to draw the whole number line?' 'Is part of the number line enough?' 'Which key points are helpful?'
- Pupils sketch the expanded section of the number line underneath and write in the numbers.
- Encourage pupils to show what they did by drawing the magnifying glass on the diagram (example available online).

Bring it together

"Pupils developed a flexible approach to informal calculations by trying different ways of showing their thinking."

Pupils apply key facts, their knowledge of components and bridging through 10 to add two-digit numbers.

Pupils apply what they have learned about the use of triads (Idea 25), bridging through 10 (Idea 56), and partial number lines (Idea 70).

Work through the example below together, discussing each stage. Then give the pupils questions to practise (see online resources).

- Write the question as an equation and on a number line. Write a '?' in place of the answer.

23 + 45 = ?

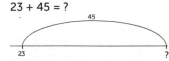

- Model the numbers using base 10 equipment and write the equations to show how the numbers are partitioned into tens and ones.

23 = 20 + 3   45 = 40 + 5

- Keep the starting number (23) intact and add second number to it, talking about the process as you do it. Add the tens first, then the ones. Record the moves on the number line and as equations.

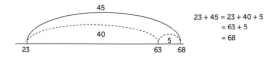

23 + 45 = 23 + 40 + 5
        = 63 + 5
        = 68

- Write the answer: 23 + 45 = 68

> **Teaching tip**
>
> If pupils find it difficult to relate the spatial representation of the number to the number line, they should model the tens and ones in the linear form as well. This relates directly to the number line.

Introducing the 100 square

"Oh, that is where a 100 square comes from! It's been on the classroom wall since Reception but I never understood what it meant." Emma aged 12

Write the number sequence to 100 on a number track, then cut it up to make a 100 square.

The 100 square is an important calculation tool. However, many pupils cannot use it effectively because they do not understand that it is a different representation of the number track. This activity turns the number track into the 100 square. It also requires pupils to focus on the alignment of numbers in the columns.

- Give each pupil a strip of paper consisting of a line of 1cm squares – there should be a few more than 100..
- Pupils write one number in each square, starting in the first square on the left with 1.
- They then cut the strip into tens and discard any numbers over 100.
- They paste the strips of ten on to a piece of paper, to create the number square, ensuring that the columns are lined up correctly (see online resource).
- Any errors the pupils have made in writing the number sequence will become obvious when they stick in the strips. They can be easily corrected: they cut out any repeated numbers and insert any that were omitted.

Demon dice

"They get really competitive about it and don't want to stop playing."

Pupils familiarise themselves with the location of numbers on the 100 square in a way which is important to them – they want to beat the opponent. Start with the basic game on a numbered 100 square. The challenge comes when they play on a blank 100 square.

Demon dice is a game for 2–4 players. The aim is to get three numbers in a row – horizontally, vertically or diagonally. You will need a 100 square (see online resources), base 10 equipment and a coloured pencil for each player.

- Players take turns to roll two 0–9 dice. They use the digits to form two numbers.
- The player writes both numbers down to help focus on the position of the digits in the number. This also prevents arguments between players if someone knocks the dice when players get overexcited.
- The player models the numbers.
- The player chooses one of the numbers and crosses out the number on the 100 square using a coloured pencil.
- Only one player may occupy each square. A player misses a turn if the possible numbers are already crossed out.
- The winner is the first player to have three crosses in a row – horizontally, vertically or diagonally.

Taking it further

Increase the complexity by introducing a third dice. Use a blank six-sided dice and write on: +1, −1, +2, −2, +10, −10.

1	2	3	4	5	6	7	8	9	10
11	12	13	14	15	16	17	18	19	20
21	22	23	24	25	26	27	28	29	30
31	32	33	34	35	36	37	38	39	40
41	42	43	44	45	46	47	48	49	50
51	52	53	54	55	56	57	58	59	60
61	62	63	64	65	66	67	68	69	70
71	72	73	74	75	76	77	78	79	80
81	82	83	84	85	86	87	88	89	90
91	92	93	94	95	96	97	98	99	100

The estimation game to 100

"It is easy to see the number with this layout."

Pupils develop a sense of the size of a quantity and a strong visual image of quantities up to 100.

Estimation, the ability to know roughly how many there are in a group of objects, is crucial to working with numbers. In this activity, players take turns to scatter objects and everyone estimates how many there are. Then the number is checked. Make sure that pupils vary the amounts so they can develop a visual image of the difference in size between quantities.

- Provide a container containing about 100 counters.
- Each player draws up a score sheet to record the estimates.
- Player A scatters a handful of counters. They allow all the players to look for a few seconds, before covering the counters with a piece of paper.
- Each player says how many counters they think there are. Everyone records all the estimates on their own score sheet.
- Player A places the counters neatly into lines of 10, arranged as an array.
- Player A counts the number of counters and everyone records the quantity on their score sheet.
- The winner is the player whose estimate is closest to the actual number of objects.

	Player A	Player B	Actual number	Winner
Round 1	54	67	64	Player B

Multiplication and division

Part 7

Times tables strategy

"Multiplication tables are much easier to learn when you understand what they mean."

This times tables strategy helps pupils understand what multiplication means so that they can quickly derive each fact in a times table by reasoning from the key facts 10n and 5n.

Many pupils find learning times tables by rote difficult because the words have no meaning for them. Adopt this times tables strategy which uses reasoning to relate all tables facts to 10 times a number (10n).

- Use equipment to demonstrate multiplication and create strong visual images.
- Keep language simple and make the meaning clear, e.g. say '6 tens' – this makes it clear that 6 is the multiplier (the number of repetitions) and ten is the multiplicand (the quantity to be repeated).
- Learn the key facts 10n and 5n.
- Use counters to show repeated groups on a multiplication mat (see Ideas 76 and 78).
- Learn the 2, 3, 4 and 6 times tables, one table at a time. Reason to derive new facts from 10n and 5n by repeated addition. Use a multiplication mat and a number line (see Ideas 76 and 77).
- Introduce the array model of multiplication and show that multiplication is commutative. Use counters and then Cuisenaire rods (see Idea 81).
- Teach the 7, 8 and 9 times tables. If pupils know the other tables there are only six new facts to learn: 7×7, 8×7, 9×7, 8×8, 9×8, 9×9.
- Link the array model to the area model of multiplication (see Idea 82).
- Teach the vocabulary of multiplication by using it in contexts. The meaning of the terms 'times', 'groups', and 'multiply by' becomes clear when the pupils model and talk about scenarios.

Five times a number

"Now I know my 10 times table and my 5 times table!"

Demonstrate 10 times a number as repeated addition and then quickly derive 5 times the number by using halving skills. All other tables can be derived from these facts by reasoning.

Check that pupils know 10 times any number up to 10 tens. Pupils should be familiar with multiplying by 10 from earlier counting and place value work (see Ideas 67, 68 and 71). Derive 5 times a number by reasoning that 5 is half of 10, so 5 times a number will be half of 10 times a number.

Demonstrate how to work out 2 times a number (see below), then pupils individually work out 5 times each number from 3 to 10. Each pupil has a multiplication mat (available online) and plenty of counters of the same size and colour.

- Discuss the design of the multiplication mat, e.g. 'How many squares does it have?' 'Why do some squares have darker edges?' 'What is half of 10?' 'Can you fold the mat to show 5 squares?'
- Use counters to model 10 twos on the mat.

- Discuss the model by posing questions, e.g. 'How many squares are there?' 'How many counters are there in each square?' 'How many counters are there altogether?'
- Figure out 5 twos by reasoning from 10 twos. Pupils explain in their own words that '5 is half of 10 so 5 twos will be half of 10 twos.' '10 twos are 20 so 5 twos will be 10.'
- Pupils adjust the model by removing counters to reflect the reasoning.

Step into repeated addition

"I can see the steps if I draw them on the number line."

Deriving times tables by applying repeated addition is much easier if you can step-count. Investigate number sequences by step-counting forwards and backwards, modelling the steps with Cuisenaire rods and recording the steps as arcs on a number line.

This activity builds pupils' confidence with step-counting which will help them quickly derive multiplication facts from the key facts. Pupils apply their knowledge of addition to work out new facts — the multiples of numbers.

Start by step-counting in tens, then in fives. Gradually work through the other times tables. Allow time for pupils to be confident with one times table before embarking on the next.

- Pupils count aloud as they step-count in tens and use Cuisenaire rods to make a linear model showing each step.
- Give pupils a number line with intervals marked but no numbers (see online resources).
- Pupils draw each step as an arc on the line and write the size of the step above each arc and the total amount after each addition below the line.

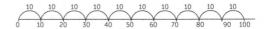

Do the same activity working backwards. Use Cuisenaire rods to make a line of 10 tens. Start at 100 at the end of line and count back in tens. Mark the arcs on the number line, starting at 100 and working back. Record the remaining amount after each 'step'.

Repeated reasoning

"There is no rote learning; only logical reasoning to make multiplication and division make sense so it is easy to figure out the facts."

Learn by reasoning from key points to quickly work out all the answers in each times tables.

Pupils often figure out multiplication facts by step-counting from the beginning of the sequence. Make the task easier by starting from convenient points (1n, 5n and 10n), which will then only involve a few repeated steps. Work on one times table at a time and do not move on until the pupil feels reasonably confident.

Pupils record their thinking as equations. Initially pupils model their thinking on a multiplication mat in order to build strong images (see Idea 76). When they are comfortable doing so, dispense with the mat but continue to write the equations. Encourage pupils to reason aloud as they model and record their thinking. It is essential that pupils use simple, clear language to focus on the quantity being repeated, In the example below, pupils are asked to work out $7 \times 4 = ?$

'7 is two more than 5 so reason from 5 fours to figure out 7 fours.
5 fours are half of 10 fours.
$10 \times 4 = 40$, so $5 \times 4 = 20$.
7 fours are 5 fours add 2 fours.
$7 \times 4 = (5 \times 4) + (2 \times 4)$
$= 20 + 8$
$= 28$

Teaching tip

Initially work on the questions that require adding on from the key points: 2x and 3x both add on from 1N; 6x and 7x add on from 5N. Then work on the questions that require counting back from the key points: subtract from 5N to calculate 4x and from 10N to calculate 8x and 9x the number.

Bonus Idea ★

Play the table filler game. This game requires pencil and paper for each player and a 1–10 dice. Select the times table (N) to practise. Players each draw up their own score sheet consisting of a list of the times tables questions in the form $1 \times N =$. Players take turns to roll the dice. They multiply N the number of times shown on the dice and write the answer on their score sheet. The winner is the first player to answer four consecutive questions.

Find the rule

"It's fun. I feel like a detective trying to figure out how the numbers are related to each other."

Continue a sequence by finding the rule that generates the sequence.

Taking it further

Give pupils plenty of practice analysing sequences and finding the rule governing them. This skill is essential for work reading scales and interpreting graphs.

Pupils need to be able to analyse a sequence of numbers to find the rule governing that sequence in order to extend it. They need to explain the rule and write it in symbolic form. Work with number sequences that are multiples of 10, 5 and 2. Once pupils are comfortable with these sequences, introduce sequences that are multiples of 3 and 4. Finally explore sequences involving multiples of 6, 7, 8, and 9 (see online resource).

Example showing multiples of 4:

- Give pupils a list of numbers in a sequence which starts from an arbitrary point in the sequence, e.g. *8, 12, 16, ___, ___, ___*
- Pupils show the numbers on a number line and use an arc to show the distance between each number.
- What is the rule? Pupils calculate the distance between each number and explain the rule. They write down the rule in the form N + (quantity).

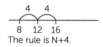

The rule is N+4.

- Pupils use the rule to generate the next three terms in the sequence and mark them on the number line.

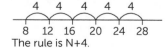

The rule is N+4.

Memorable times

"Talking about the cards helps me remember where the one I want is hiding."

Play this variant of the memory game to learn multiplication facts and introduce the concept of factors of numbers.

Memorable times is a variant of The memory game (Ideas 20 and 33). It is a game for two players and requires a pack of multiplication question cards and answer cards in a different colour (see online resources). Players seek matching pairs of cards.

Focus on one times table at a time until pupils are reasonably confident, and then introduce a few more tables. It is difficult to play with very large numbers of cards, so limit play to a maximum of four times tables at a time. And only do that once pupils are confident!

- Players check that they have all the cards by putting the questions cards in sequence and matching the answer cards.
- Shuffle the cards and place them face down on the table in a structured arrangement.
- The first player turns up a question card, reads the table question and says the answer they are looking for, e.g. they turn up 5 x 5 and say: '5 fives make 25.'
- The same player then turns up an answer card. If the cards are a matching pair, the player keeps them and has another turn.
- If the player does not find a matching pair, they read the number on the answer card and say what multiplication makes that number, e.g. they turn up 30: the player says: '30 is made of 6 fives.' They turn the cards face down and the next player has a turn.
- The winner is the player with the most cards when they have all been paired up.

Teaching tip

It is very important that cards always remain in the same position on the table. Maximum learning takes place if pupils read what is written on the cards and discuss the relationships between the questions and answers. Take this a step further by asking pupils to stop occasionally and recap which cards have been turned up, and by whom, *before* having a turn. This helps improve memory skills as it makes all players concentrate on all the cards as they are played.

Taking it further

Practise factors and lay down foundations for division by playing the same game but this time turning up an answer card first and work out the question, e.g. player turns up 45 and says: '45 is made of 9 fives.' OR 'There are 9 fives in 45.' This activity is helpful for building confidence with the more difficult tables.

The array model

"I am so glad that I made sure the pupils had plenty of time making arrays. It is has really helped them to understand long multiplication and division."

Explore the concept of multiplication as an array and demonstrate the commutative property of multiplication.

Put counters in rows and columns to form a rectangle. This model is called an array. The strong visual image makes the inverse relationship between multiplication and division clear.

- Roll two dice numbered 1 to 6. Use the numbers to write a multiplication question, e.g. 5 x 3.
- Read the question in the form: '5 threes.' This makes it clear that each row will contain 3 counters.
- Model the question. Put 3 counters into each row. Discuss the arrangement. Draw the array and write the equation, e.g.

5 x 3 = 15

Multiplication is commutative: changing the order in which the numbers are multiplied does not change the result, i.e. a x b = b x a. Explore this equivalence. Write down and discuss the two possible multiplication questions, e.g. 5 x 3 and 3 x 5. Compare the models and check that both have the same number of counters. Draw the arrays and write the equations, e.g.

5 x 3 = 15

3 x 5 = 15

The area model

"Doing it this way made it so easy to calculate the area of shapes when we started doing measurement."

Link the array model of multiplication to the area model and make the commutative property of multiplication clear.

Use 1 cm² cubes and squared paper, then Cuisenaire rods, to find out why multiplying the number of counters in a row by the number of rows gives the area of a rectangle. This idea builds on the array model (Idea 81).

Taking it further

This activity shows what it means to find the area of a shape. When you calculate the area of a shape you are working out how many squares of a specified unit of measurement will fit into the space.

- Roll two dice numbered 1 to 6. Use the numbers to write two multiplication questions, e.g. 4 x 3 and 3 x 4. Say the questions: '4 threes and 3 fours.'
- Use cubes to model the question. Step count to calculate the answer.
- Draw a diagram on 1 cm² squared paper.

4 x 3 = 12   3 x 4 = 12

- Use Cuisenaire rods to show that 4 x 3 = 3 x 4. Put out 4 threes in a line with 3 fours.

- Use rods to make the area model, e.g.

- Turn the model of 3 fours and place it over the model of 4 threes to prove that they occupy exactly the same area.

Boxing clever

"The area model morphs seamlessly into the box method for recording multiplication with larger numbers."

Extend the area model of multiplication to two-digit numbers. This leads directly to the box method, also known as the grid method, for recording multiplication calculations.

The box method uses partitioning to build on the area model of multiplication to calculate with larger numbers. The calculation takes place in clearly defined stages. The products of each part of the calculation are recorded in a table comprised of 'boxes'.

Pupils use base 10 equipment to model the question then they draw a diagram and record their thinking. Start by multiplying a single digit and a two-digit number.

Ask all pupils to work through this example independently: 3 x 16 = ?.

- Read the question: '3 sixteens make what?'
- Partition 16 and model it as a row of one ten and six ones.
- Continue the model to show 3 x 16 as an array: three rows with 16 in each row e.g.

- Draw the box diagram as shown below with a multiplication sign at the top left: 16 is partitioned into 10 and 6 so these numbers are written above the boxes as shown; there are three repetitions, or rows, so the number 3 is written on the left hand side, e.g.

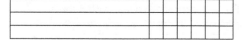

- Perform the calculation for each part and write the product in the relevant box:
  3 x 10 = 30 and 3 x 6 =18
- Add the quantity in each box to find the total. Pupils check the answer against their model.
- Write the addition as an equation:
  30 + 18 = 48
- Write the answer to the original question:
  3 x 16 = 48.

```
×  10 + 6
3 | 30 | 18 |
30 + 18 = 48
  3 × 16 = 48
```

Do further examples, e.g. 4 x 13, 5 x 27, 6 x 34

When pupils can confidently calculate with this form, work with two-digit numbers multiplied by two-digit numbers, e.g. 13 x 24 = ? For practical purposes it is best to restrict the multiplier to numbers from 11 to 19 to avoid too many rows making the model unwieldy. Both numbers are partitioned into tens and ones so there will be four boxes, e.g.

```
×  20 + 4
10 |    |    |
 3 |    |    |
```

- Pupils calculate the quantity in each box and record them.
- They add the number in each row and record it, then add these totals.
- It is essential that pupils record each stage of their thinking clearly.

```
×  20 + 4
10 | 260 | 40 |    200 + 40 = 240
 3 |  60 | 12 |     60 + 12 =  72
240 + 72 = 312
 13 × 24 = 312
```

Do further examples, e.g. 12 x 34, 15 x 43.

Fair shares

"Some quantities can be arranged in several different ways. For others there are only two ways. And there is only one way to arrange one."

Pupils are in for some surprises as they explore the different ways quantities can be split into equal-sized groups (with no remainders).

Teaching tip

Use paper baking cases as the cups. These are inexpensive and they are shallow enough to easily see how many counters are in each cup.

A completed table is available online, including all factors up to 30.

Pupils put counters into containers to discover how many different ways each number can be divided, with no remainders.

Each pupil carries out their own investigation. They should start by investigating numbers to 12. So, each pupil will have 12 cups and 12 counters. The rules are:

• same number of counters in each cup
• no remainders.

They draw a chart with three columns headed: 'Number'; 'How many cups?'; 'How many counters in each cup?' (see online resources).

• Write 1 on the chart in the 'Number' column.
• Take one counter. How many ways can you arrange one counter?
• The only possibility is one cup containing one counter. Record this on the chart. Rule off as there is only one possibility.
• Write 2 on the chart in the 'Number' column.
• Take two counters. How many ways can you arrange two counters?
• Model the arrangements and describe them, e.g. 'I can have 1 cup with 2 counters in it. Or there can be 2 cups with 1 counter in each cup.' Record the findings on the chart. Rule off.
• Continue to systematically explore each number up to 12.
• Pupils can work in pairs, or as a whole class, to discuss their findings.

Groupings

"Factors are easy when you arrange counters into equal-sized groups."

Discover why numbers are prime numbers and square numbers.

When you list the ways that numbers can be spilt into equal-sized groups, some intriguing patterns emerge. Many pupils are afraid of factors so use the word 'groupings' to start with. Make sure they have grasped the concept explored in Idea 84 that each number can be arranged as groups in a limited number of ways. Then explain that when a number divides into another number, it is called a factor of that number.

- Use the information from the chart in Idea 84 to list all the factors for each number up to 12 (see online resources).
- Count how many factors there are for each number and write the total number of factors.
- Analyse the list to find what the number of factors can tell you about the quantities, e.g. how many numbers have one factor? Which numbers have two factors? Which numbers have three factors? Which numbers have an even number of factors? Which numbers have an odd number of factors?

Taking it further

Investigate factors of larger numbers, particularly 24 and 60. Discuss why these were chosen for measuring time intervals. Why was 360 a good number to choose to measure the degrees of turn in a circle?

Number	Factors	How many factors?
1	1	1
2	1, 2	2
3	1, 3	2
4	1, 2, 4	3
5	1, 5	2
6	1, 2, 3, 6	4
7	1, 7	2
8	1, 2, 4, 8	4
9	1, 3, 9	3
10	1, 2, 5, 10	4
11	1, 11	2
12	1, 2, 3, 4, 6, 12	6

Hailstone numbers

"Easy to do. Impossible to prove that the sequence will always end the same way."

Pupils identify odd and even numbers and practise multiplying by 3 and dividing by 2. They create an intriguing number sequence in a routine summarised as 'halve or triple plus one'.

Teaching tip

If you want to keep pupils busy, ask them to start with 27. It produces the longest sequence for any number below 100.

Pupils carry out a procedure to produce the next term in a sequence. The values in the sequence bounce up and down, which is why they are sometimes called hailstone numbers.

- Pick a number between 5 and 10.
- Is the number even? Divide it by 2.
- Is the number odd? Multiply by 3 and add 1.
- Look at your answer and repeat the process.
- Continue until you realise you can go no further, e.g. for the starting number 5:
- 5 is odd: $(3 \times 5) + 1 = \textbf{16}$
  16 is even: $16 \div 2 = \textbf{8}$
  8 is even: $8 \div 2 = \textbf{4}$
  4 is even: $4 \div 2 = \textbf{2}$
  2 is even: $2 \div 2 = \textbf{1}$
  1 is an odd number: $(3 \times 1) + 1 = \textbf{4}$
  4 is even: $4 \div 2 = \textbf{2}$
  2 is even: $2 \div 2 = \textbf{1}$
- Draw up a table of sequences obtained from the starting numbers 5, 6, 7, 8, 9, 10.
- What do you notice? (The last three numbers in every sequence will be 4, 2, 1.)

Make sure that pupils generate plenty of sequences of their own before drawing their attention to the 4, 2, 1 end pattern. Does the procedure always end in 1? This is the Collatz conjecture: no matter which number you start with, you eventually reach 1. However, no one has managed to prove that this is true.

Try the same activity with some two-digit numbers.

Bonus Idea ★

It is useful to show pupils that something simple may not be as straightforward as it seems. Getting a result is one part of the process, explaining why it is true is quite another. So far no one knows whether hailstone numbers are simply a bit of fun, or will lead to a new branch of mathematics.

Place value

Part 8

It's all in a name

"It can be frustrating as pupils struggle to keep the ones in place. Persevere. They will never forget the image of 100 ones in a hundred square."

Make sure that pupils understand why the 100 square is called the one hundred square. It is not just a name; it describes it exactly.

Teaching tip

Do not use ten sticks that are calibrated into ones. This obscures the point of having ten sticks as it encourages pupils to focus on the ones, rather than seeing the ten as a single quantity representing 10 ones.

Bonus Idea ★

Introduce measurement with a purpose by asking older pupils to make their own 100 squares and tens sticks from recycled cardboard. (It is not practical to make 1cm³ cubes.) This task emphasises the importance of measuring accurately.

Pupils investigated the relationship between tens and ones in Idea 53 when dealing with the principle of exchange, and in Idea 60 with the value of digits. Now they explore the relationships between tens and ones and the 100 square.

Give each pupil a blank 100 square measuring 10cm x 10cm (available online) but do not tell them the size. Provide plenty of base 10 tens and ones.

- **How many ones fit in the square?** Pupils use 1cm³ cubes to work out how many fit into the square. Many pupils find it very difficult to place the pieces in the space neatly. Encourage them to persevere. Do not do it for them. Developing their visuo-perceptual and motor skills is an important part of learning and gaining a sense of how large the quantity 100 is. They talk about what they are doing and write the result. The image of 100 ones inside the square makes it clear what the term '100 square' means.
- **How many tens fit in the square?** Pupils do the same exercise using tens rods. It is important that they talk about what they are doing and write the result in order to produce the strong visual image that 10 tens make 100.

A sense of size

"Investigation is the best way to learn. Place value makes sense when you see that HTO actually does mean hundreds, tens and ones."

Large numbers make sense when pupils model the relationship between hundreds, tens and ones.

The principle of exchange is the foundation of place value. Too often teachers dispense with equipment when working with bigger numbers. This is a pity. Base 10 equipment makes the meaning clear: the relative size of the pieces of equipment equates to the place value position.

In this activity, pupils discover that it is easier and more efficient to deal with large quantities of objects if they are structured into groups. Model large numbers in a line of ones, then exchange the ones for hundreds, tens and ones. Work in pairs to encourage discussion. Provide plenty of cubes to use as counters.

- Tell pupils to put out a line of cubes to show the number 234. (Do not write it on the board.)
- Count to check for accuracy.
- Discuss whether there is an easier way to model 234, e.g. ask: 'Can you put the counters into groups? What size groups can you use? What is the most efficient way of grouping them? Can you show cut-off points for the groups in the line? Can you exchange groups of ones for tens? Can you exchange groups of tens for hundreds?'
- Ask pupils to model 234 using hundreds, tens and ones. They draw a diagram and say how many hundreds, tens and ones there are.
- They write the number and its composition:
  234 = 2 hundreds and 3 tens and 4 ones
  234 = 200 + 30 + 4

Three-digit swap

"How many different numbers can you make with three different digits?"

Place value is easy once you realise that hundreds, tens and ones are a way of making numbers easy to visualise.

The place value structure makes it possible to represent any quantity from the minuscule to the massive by using only the ten digits: 0, 1, 2, 3, 4, 5, 6, 7, 8, 9. The value of each digit depends on its position in the number.

The place value structure is often shown as a series of columns headed H T O. Too often pupils interpret the digit in each column in isolation; make the meaning clear by building numbers. This idea builds on Idea 88.

Provide base 10 equipment: hundred squares, tens rods and ones cubes. Each pupil has a place value mat which is an A4 piece of paper with three columns headed H T O, and three digit cards labelled 1, 2, 3. Pupils work individually.

- Place the number cards next to each other in any order to make a three-digit number.
- Read the number.
- Use the base 10 equipment to model the number on the place value mat.
- Describe the number and draw a diagram of it.
- Write the number and the equation to show what the number represents.

$$123 = 100 + 20 + 3$$

- Rearrange the number cards to form a new number, then model, draw and write it.

Zero holds the place

"Zero is a really powerful number. It keeps the other numbers in their place."

Zero plays a very important role in the place value system. Use equipment to model numbers that include zero as a place holder.

Zero occupies a place to show that there is no quantity of a particular value in a multi-digit number. Unfortunately, some pupils think that zero means nothing and that it can be ignored. In this activity, pupils investigate the essential role that zero plays. This activity extends Idea 89; now each number contains a zero.

Provide base 10 equipment: hundred squares, tens rods and ones cubes, and digit cards 0 to 5.

- Pupils draw a place value mat – an A4 sheet of paper with three column headings: H T O.
- Give each pupil three digit cards with a different number on each; ensure one card has a 0 (zero).
- Pupils place the cards next to each other to make a three-digit number.
- Pupils model the number on the place value mat using base 10 equipment under the appropriate headings. Give pupils an extra 0 (zero) digit card to place in the space on the model where there is no base 10 equipment to show that zero holds the place, e.g.

H	T	O
☐☐	0	▫▫▫

203 = 2 hundreds, 0 tens and 3 ones

- Pupils discuss the model. They draw a diagram, write the number and show what it represents.

Teaching tip

Limit digit cards to the numbers 0 to 5 for practical purposes as the models become unwieldy where large quantities of 100 squares are required. Of course, allow pupils to model larger numbers if they are keen to do so.

Zero wars

"Play around with zero to help you win the war."

Pupils need plenty of practice in reading and modelling numbers that include a zero.

Taking it further

Emphasise the importance of zero as a place holder by asking pupils to write their numbers on a number line. This helps them see that there is a difference between zero as a place holder, and zero as a point at the beginning of a number line.

Extend the game 'Card wars' (Idea 68) to larger numbers and include a zero. This competitive game encourages pupils to pay close attention to the role of zero as they build different numbers. They are allowed to place zero at the beginning of the number, although convention dictates that we do not write it as it is not necessary.

Supply four sets of digit cards 0–9 and a size card marked 'largest' on one side and 'smallest' on the other. Each player needs a plentiful supply of base 10 tens and ones, and a zero place holder card.

- Give each player three digit cards, ensuring everyone has one 0 (zero) card. They place them face down in front of them.
- The dealer decides whether the smallest or the largest number will win and turns the size card to show the appropriate word ('smallest' or 'largest').
- Players make a number out of their three digit cards and then model it using hundreds, tens and ones and a zero place holder card.
- The person with the largest or smallest number, as appropriate, says: 'I have the [largest/smallest] number.'
- At the end of each round, the winning player collects all the cards.
- The winner is the player with the most cards when they have all been played.

Rolling towards 999

"Strategy, calculation and a bit of luck all come into this quick game."

Pupils apply the principle of exchange as they accumulate quantities to see who can get closest to 999.

It is essential that pupils can exchange 10 ones for 1 ten, and 10 tens for 1 hundred when required. This competitive game gives purposeful practice in adding three-digit numbers. Pupils develop confidence in modelling three-digit numbers and discuss the exchanges in a way that transfers easily to the formal written methods.

This game for two–four players requires plenty of base 10 hundreds, tens and ones, three dice numbered 0 to 9, and a pencil and paper for each player. Each player will have five turns. The aim is to achieve a total score as close to 999 as possible. Players take turns to roll the dice and record the digits.

- On their first turn, each player rolls the three dice and decides which three-digit number to make.
- They write down their number and model it using base 10 equipment.
- On each subsequent turn, players add hundreds, tens and ones to their model. They place the new quantity below the original number. Then they carry out any necessary exchanges. Each player must explain what they are doing on each turn.
- If a turn takes the player past 999, they forfeit their score and start again from zero.
- The winner is the person who is closest to 999 after all players have had their five turns.

Teaching tip

Encourage pupils to apply their knowledge of rounding to help them work out the approximate size of the possible numbers to make on each turn.

Taking it further

Each pupil starts with 999 made from 9 hundred squares, 9 tens rods and 9 ones. They take turns to roll the dice and remove the chosen quantity from the model. Pupils may have to decompose quantities on the model before they can subtract the required amount. If a turn would take them past zero, they must start again. The winner is the person who is closest to zero after five turns.

Clapping cue game

"You have to be alert and listening for this quick filler activity that everyone enjoys."

Listen carefully to work out whether to count in ones, tens or hundreds. One clap means count in ones, two claps indicates count in tens, and three claps signals count in hundreds.

Teaching tip

Be careful to do this activity with pupils who are at a similar level of expertise. A pupil who has difficulty should not be expected to take part in the class activity. They will need plenty of individual practice working with a bead string (see Ideas 28 and 66) in order to develop fluency.

Taking it further

Pupils who are proficient at counting, may like to try the more difficult task of switching between counting forwards and backwards. This requires another signal – a hand pointing up or down. Introducing a visual cue alongside the audio cues requires pupils to pay even closer attention. Now the teacher claps and points, e.g. two claps followed by a hand pointing up means count forwards in tens; three claps and a hand pointing down means reverse direction and count backwards in hundreds.

Resist the temptation to make this a race. The aim is to develop confidence and accuracy. Counting in steps of 100 is fast because the steps are large; ten is a medium step and one is a slow step. The class works together.

Count to 100

Practise the technique by doing slow and medium counting only at first, up to 100:

- one clap means count in ones from the present number
- two claps means switch to counting in tens, continuing from the last number.

Teacher says a number and claps once. Pupils count on. Teacher claps twice. Pupils count in tens. Continue to switch between counting in ones and tens until pupils reach 100.

Count to 999

Introduce the signal for counting in hundreds:

- three claps means count in hundreds.

Start at 100 and do the same activity. Vary the counting sequence to include counting in ones, tens and hundreds.

Counting back

The same rules apply. Start at 100 and count back in ones or tens. When pupils are confident, start at 999 and count back in ones, tens and hundreds.

The rule of HTO

"Place value really is as simple as HTO once you realise that the pattern goes on repeating."

Reading and writing very large numbers is easy once you grasp the rule of HTO: the three categories hundreds, tens and ones (HTO) are repeated within larger categories – thousands, millions, billions, trillions . . . and on . . . and on.

Use a place value grid and digit cards to make it clear that the thousand category also includes HTO positions (see online resources). This simple activity can transform a pupil's attitude within minutes when they realise they can read big numbers.

- Give pupils a place value grid with six columns headed H T O H T O.
- Discuss how you can distinguish between the two groups of HTO: write the word 'Thousands' across the top of the first group of HTO.
- Pupils point to each column and read the titles: 'hundred thousands, ten thousands, thousands, hundreds, tens, ones'.
- Place three digit cards under HTO in the thousands category, e.g. 534. Cover up the word 'Thousands' and the empty columns. Pupils read the number.
- Expose the empty columns and the 'Thousands' heading. Pupils now read the number as five hundred and thirty four thousand. Zeros are required to hold the empty places (see Idea 90).

Thousands					
H	T	O	H	T	O
5	3	4	0	0	0

- Replace the zeros with three more digit cards in the HTO columns to make a six-digit number and ask the pupils to read the whole number.

Taking it further

Teach millions in the same way. Provide a grid with nine columns headed HTO HTO HTO and discuss how the groups can be distinguished. The new group will be the millions category.

Bonus Idea ★

For the wow factor, ask pupils to model a six-digit number. They will have to make their own equipment for the ten thousand rod and the hundred thousand square. Do this using discarded cardboard. The size of a cuboid representing ten 1,000 cubes and one hundred 1,000 cubes makes a dramatic display.

Getting formal: addition

"I made a model of the numbers and then the written method turned out to be exactly like it!"

Relate standard written methods to models on the place value grid. Pupils apply their knowledge of place value and the principle of exchange and write numbers to show what they are doing.

Establish the habit of working out an approximate answer, or estimate, before starting the formal calculation. This acts as a quick benchmark against which to check the answer. Having a rough idea of the expected result is an important part of problem solving in real life and it is good to ingrain the idea early on.

Do not teach the procedure for formal addition as a set of rules; anxious pupils cannot remember them. Help pupils to understand the addition algorithm, sometimes called the column method, by showing them how to derive the process from work with concrete materials. The model of the question is an exact representation of the standard written methods and makes the meaning of the value of each digit explicit.

- Write the addition question under HTO column headings.
- Work out a rough estimate for the answer by rounding both numbers to the nearest 100 and then adding them.
- Build the numbers on the place value grid.
- Discuss the process of adding the quantities on the model, including any exchanges if necessary.
- Draw a diagram to show the process.
- Write the calculation in columns and show clearly any amount that has been exchanged.

Taking it further

Do plenty of examples. When pupils are proficient with three-digit numbers, give them four-digit numbers to work with. It is not possible to model numbers that are larger than 9,999.

HTO   Estimate: 200 + 400 = 600

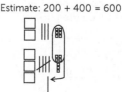

Getting formal: subtraction

"Now I understand why the written method works. It is like the model."

Model subtraction to make the formal written method crystal clear. The written account exactly describes the moves on the model.

Formal subtraction is based on the concept of taking away. Use base 10 equipment to model a number, then discuss and record the steps required to take an amount away from it. Many pupils are greatly relieved to find that all they have to do is explain what they are looking at.

No decomposition

- Write the subtraction question under HTO column headings.
- Work out a rough estimate for the answer by rounding both numbers to the nearest 100 and then doing the subtraction.
- Draw a diagram to show the initial quantity and model the question. There is only one quantity to model. This is the initial amount.
- Start with the ones column and take away the specified quantity on the model.
- Show this on the diagram and write the result.
- Continue the calculation.

With decomposition

Repeat the exercise with a question requiring decomposition between the tens and the ones. What is recorded in the written form will be an exact representation of the model.

Teaching tip
Once pupils can confidently handle decomposition, generate numbers using dice or cards. This adds an element of fun rather than working through a list of examples.

$$\begin{array}{l} \text{H T O} \\ 5\,{}^{8}\!\cancel{9}\,{}^{1}3 \\ \underline{1\ 2\ 8} - \\ 4\ 6\ 5 \end{array}$$

Estimate: 600 − 100 = 500

The stubborn number

"Solving a puzzle makes addition and subtraction so much more fun."

One number keeps coming up. Get pupils puzzling over it and practising addition and subtraction in the process.

Teaching tip

Model the question with base 10 equipment for extra impact.

Make sure that pupils set out each subtraction and addition calculation in the standard written form.

Pupils need plenty of practice adding and subtracting three-digit numbers. This activity will have them scratching their heads and looking for the exception. In this mathematical puzzle, pupils choose their own number and follow a set calculation procedure. Whatever the starting number, the answer is always the same.

- Take any three-digit number in which the first and last digits differ by two or more, e.g. 642.
- Reverse the number.
- Now subtract the smaller of the two numbers from the larger number.
- Take the answer and reverse it to make a new number.
- Add the answer and the new number together.
- What number to you get?
- Do several more examples.
- What do you notice about the results? (The answer is always 1,089.)

$$
\begin{array}{r}
642 \\
246\ - \\
\hline
396
\end{array}
\qquad
\begin{array}{r}
396 \\
693\ + \\
\hline
1\ 089
\end{array}
$$

The constant number

"The answer comes as a surprise – time after time!"

Intrigue pupils with this subtraction activity. It is known as Kaprekar's routine after the mathematician who first discovered a rather special number. Don't tell the pupils any more; see if they can find the number.

Practise standard method of subtraction. Pupils investigate a variety of numbers using a fixed routine to discover something surprising (see online resources).

- Write any four-digit number that uses four different digits.
- Rearrange the digits to form the largest possible number.
- Rearrange the digits to form the smallest possible number.
- Subtract the smaller number from the bigger number.
- Take the result and repeat the process.
- Continue to do this until you think you've found something that interests you. (Eventually they will find that the number 6,174 repeats.)
- Note that if there is a zero in a number, the smaller number will be a three-digit number. (You can put the zero at the beginning if it helps to keep track of the digits.)

Don't spoil the surprise by telling the pupils what they are going to find out. The constant number also has a built in error alert. If pupils make a mistake in calculation they will not reach a conclusion within seven iterations. (An iteration is a step in a repeated process.) The pupil will then need to go back and check the calculations. A quick way to do this is to add the smaller number and the result to see if it makes the larger number.

Teaching tip

The number 6,174 is called 'Kaprekar's constant'. Ask pupils to consider a variety of numbers and track how many iterations (repeated procedures) are needed to reach 6,174.

Taking it further

Explore four-digit numbers in which some digits are repeated. Try each of these variations: a four-digit number in which any two digits are the same; a four-digit number in which any three digits are the same. The answer will always be 6,174.

Bonus Idea ★

There is another curious characteristic of the numbers in Kaprekar's routine. The result of each iteration is a multiple of 9. Check this by dividing each number by 9. This highlights the inverse relationship between multiplication and division.

Getting formal: multiplication

"I'm so glad I did all the multiplication modelling and understood the box method. Now I can see how to do formal multiplication."

Teach long multiplication by reasoning not by rote. Link the box method of multiplication (Idea 83) and the standard addition method (Idea 95).

Teaching tip

Give pupils plenty of practice in switching from the box method to the formal method before they dispense with the box method. Allow pupils to use base 10 to check their answers.

Too often long multiplication is introduced as a series of steps; the meaning is lost in a flurry of instructions which pupils often 'misremember'. However, if pupils understand the reasoning underlying the written method, they will be able to use the standard algorithm, and they will have a sense of the quantity the answer represents. The trick is to make sure they are fully prepared. Pupils need to be comfortable partitioning numbers, to understand place value and be able to use the box method. Don't rush them into long multiplication until they are confident with these underlying concepts.

Work through an example to show that long multiplication merely involves changing the way that the box method is recorded. It is advisable first to revise the box method to remind pupils how it works (Idea 83). Then, start by multiplying a single-digit and a two-digit number, e.g. 3 x 42.

- Write the question 3 x 42 = ? at the top of the page.
- Mark two sections on the recording sheet headed 'box method', and 'long multiplication'.
- Draw the diagram for the calculation in the box method.

- Show how the written method follows the same structure but the box is omitted. The two-digit number is written at the top, and the single-digit number below it. Numbers are written in the appropriate place value columns. Draw a line under the question.

Box method   Long multiplication method

```
  ×  40 + 2              H T O
                           4 2
3 |    |   |                 3 ×
                         ‾‾‾‾‾‾‾
```

- Calculate 3 x 40 in the box method and record the answer.
- Show how 3 x 40 is recorded below the line in the written method.
- Point to the answers in the written method and compare them with the answers in the box method.

Box method   Long multiplication method

```
  ×  40 + 2              H T O
                           4 2
3 | 120 | 6 |               3 ×
                         ‾‾‾‾‾‾‾
                         1 2 0
                             6
```

- What is the next step in the box method? Discuss this.
- Compare the results in the written method to the formal addition method. Write the addition sign to make it clear that the next stage is to add the products.

Box method   Long multiplication method

```
  ×  40 + 2              H T O
                           4 2
3 | 120 | 6 |               3 ×
                         ‾‾‾‾‾‾‾
  120 + 6 = 126          1 2 0
                             6 +
                         ‾‾‾‾‾‾‾
                         1 2 6
```

Taking it further

This method transfers directly to long multiplication with larger numbers. First multiply two-digit by two-digit numbers, then move on to multi-digit numbers. Make sure that pupils talk about what they are doing, and why.

119

Multiplication puzzles

"How cool is that! Multiplication does create surprises!"

Give pupils practice with a purpose to hone their long multiplication skills.

Intrigue pupils with these multiplication questions. Find some unexpected results!

- **Puzzle 1**: Multiplying numbers that contain only the digit 1 results in an interesting pattern. A number which is composed of the repeated digit 1 is called a 'repunit' number, which is short for repeated unit. Use long multiplication to work out the following:

  11 x 11
  111 x 111
  1111 x 1111
  11111 x 11111

Write the answers underneath each other. What do you notice? (The answers are palindromes that follow a distinctive pattern: 121, then 12321, then 1234321 and so on.)

- **Puzzle 2**: 142,857 is such an interesting number that it even has its own Wikipedia page. Do the following calculations and write the answers underneath each other. Compare the answers.

  1 x 142,857 =   *4 x 142,857 =*
  2 x 142,857 =   *5 x 142,857 =*
  3 x 142,857 =   *6 x 142,857 =*

Pupils will notice that the digits in each answer are the same, though each answer starts from a different place in the sequence.

Then work out 7 x 142,857. The answer of 999,999 is unexpected! (Investigating the reason for this will have to wait until pupils can handle fractions and recurring decimals.)